Testimonials for Robin's Parent Power Presentation

"Every parent deserves the opportunity to experience Parent Power! Robin's presentation was absolutely wonderful, packed with outstanding, effective strategies and tools that any parent can implement immediately, with instant results. Robin brings personal experience, professional expertise, humor, and awareness to assist parents with the ongoing challenges we face. She has a concise way of presenting the challenges *and* providing the solutions or strategies to build positive relationships. Parenting can sometimes be so overwhelming. When I left Robin's class I felt so much better about myself and my ability to parent more consciously. Robin reminded me that being a parent is an awesome gift!"

   - Debbie Burns
   Director, Peace Center

"After attending Robin's parenting seminar, I was excited to go home and try out what I had learned. The following morning, I gave my three-year-old two choices for breakfast, and I amazingly had no resistance from him. I had a smile from ear to ear. It's been a week now. I have followed through with giving him choices, and I no longer have control issues with him. I'm spreading the word to all of my friends, and it's worked for them too. This seminar should be a prerequisite for having children (like child birthing classes). Thanks Robin!!!!!"

   - Kim

"Robin gave us the tools and training to prepare us for our most important job, and we are more effective, better parents for it. The unexpected benefit is the effect it has had on our own relationship. We feel like more of a united parenting team rather than a divided and conquered household. The children have responded well to the new approach. Thank you, Robin!"

   - Andy

Go Take A Bath!

A Powerful Self-Care Approach to Extraordinary Parenting

Robin M. Kevles-Necowitz, M.Ed., LPC

Enjoy the Journey!

Warmly,

"There is no need to go to India or anywhere else to find peace. You will find that deep place of silence right in your room, your garden or even your bathtub."

– Elisabeth Kubler-Ross

In Gratitude

To my parents: Thank you for giving me life. I feel forever grateful for my life experiences with both of you. It wasn't easy for any of us, but we emerged triumphant. Mom, I miss you. I feel grateful that before your death you knew that despite our years of conflict, I found peace, love, joy, and gratitude in our relationship. I know how you delighted in my breaking the cycle of pain in this generation. Dad, I appreciate and feel your pride in the woman, wife, and mother I have become. I love you very much.

Ross Kevles: I couldn't possibly ask for a better brother. There is no one I would have preferred growing up with. I love you so much. You are an amazing man, father, brother, and officer in the United States Navy. You are hilarious, kind, and supportive. We will always be bonded by our childhood experience. I love having you as a brother and a friend.

Larry Necowitz: What can I say? Thanks for the hours and hours you put in to help me birth this baby. I am so glad I healed myself enough BEFORE I met you so I could be healthy enough to build a loving relationship with such an amazing man. You are the greatest husband and father I could have hoped for. Thank you for everything you do to support me. I know I'm high maintenance and a lot to manage, but you do it with grace. Thank you for loving me so much. I love you right back, babe.

Arli and Zoe Necowitz: You light up my life. You are my greatest teachers. I am so incredibly proud of you. Just watching how you move in this world makes me want to be a better human being every day. You are amazing, beautiful souls, and I feel BLESSED beyond any words I can write to have been given the privilege to be your mom. This book would not have been possible without all your love and lessons.

Nugget Necowitz, my precious dog: You came into our lives at the perfect time. Your love is a great comfort to us all, and I truly enjoyed having you by my feet as I wrote this book. I love you.

Aunt Harriet Zeff: Thank you for being my biggest cheerleader. You always dream big dreams for me. Thank you for the wise counsel over the years and for your constant warmth and loving presence. I love you.

Aunt Eileen Snyder: Thank you for keeping me laughing about our family and always rejoicing in my successes. Your amazing sense of humor always tickles me when I need it the most. I love you.

Beth Hoffman: That you for giving me the privilege of a lifetime. Being part of the team that ushered your beautiful son into the world is among my greatest experiences of all time. I feel so blessed to have been given such a high honor. Your strength and focus were humbling and awe inspiring. My deep prayer for you is that you will take the ideas presented in this book and integrate them into your parenting journey from the very beginning. You are in a unique position to learn from the start that bathing in a pool of self-care is the key to parenting success and enjoyment. I love you so much and thank you for your trust and confidence in me. I look forward to watching you flourish as a "self-care-focused" mom.

Jill Hammer and Amy Valerio: You are my go-to parenting posse. I have deep respect for both of you as women, mothers, and friends. You are the people I turn to when I need a recipe, life advice, to cry, or to share a funny story. Thank God for WWAD (Amy), and your clear, direct, honest feedback (Jill). You both always point me in the right direction when I feel lost in the parenting mire. Thanks, ladies. I don't know what I would do without you. I am so grateful to have such amazing friends.

Maureen McCormac: Thank you for being my laughing buddy. If ever I need a good time, I know exactly where to go. Having you around is like having a party in my pocket. Everyone should have a friend who can make them laugh till they cry. If I didn't have you to turn to when I need a mommy vacation or a laugh, I don't know where I'd be. I'm sure I'd be rocking in a corner somewhere. I feel lucky to have found you. Despite our many differences, you are a dear forever friend for whom I am eternally grateful. I love you.

Dave and Michelle O'Brien: Who would have thought when we met at Burger King at age fourteen that we would still be such dear friends all these years later? I feel deep love for and from you. Thank you for being such loyal, loving friends. You are the people I would call at 4:00 a.m. if I ever needed to be reminded I was loved, and I know I would never need to worry that I was intruding. How can I express my love for friends like that?

Lori Rice-Spring: It is such a comfort having someone else in the world who thinks like me! I feel so blessed to have met you all those years ago in graduate school. I am so happy that despite the distance, we manage to stay in touch and find time to see each other on a regular basis. Thank you for being a great friend and sounding board over the years. Your deep understanding of me, kindness, brilliance, and love have always been a great support. I love you.

Nirbhe Kaur and Mahan Rishi Khalsa: Thank you for reminding me how important it is to BREATHE. And for always being such a warm and loving presence in my life. Your calm, loving, peaceful energy has had a profound impact on me. Your influence is more than you can possibly know. You will find many of the lessons that you have taught me over the years peppered throughout this book. I love you both and can't thank you enough. Sat Nam.

Leigh Tilden, my dear therapist and advisor: Wow. You have been my great teacher of the concept "manage your own anxiety" over the course of many years (I'm a slow learner). Thank you for always refocusing me back to *me* when I want to complain about others and how I've been WRONGED in some ridiculous way. I know I don't always like what you have to say, but I am deeply appreciative of your unwavering commitment to me and my emotional growth. I respect your truth-telling, storytelling, humor, and courage. My husband thanks you. My friends thank you. My clients thank you. My kids DEFINITELY thank you. And if this book is successful, the whole world will thank you too. I love you.

JoEllen Werthman: You have been a source of light and love in my life. You have been a great spiritual teacher and advisor. You always redirect me back to God, and I appreciate that immensely. It is so comforting to have someone in my life who truly understands and accepts me. I feel seen, known, and enveloped in God's love when I am with you. I love you and feel forever grateful for you.

Jerry Manas: Thank you for all your help guiding me through this process from the very beginning until the bittersweet end. Your unwavering support, endless patience, and HUGE heart have helped me tremendously. I can't thank you enough for your kindness, knowledge, and especially your generosity. I am forever grateful.

Jack Tatar: Thank you for meeting with me before I even started this project to help me understand what was required. If we had not met that day for lunch, this book would never have been written. Thank you for taking your time to assist and encourage me. I greatly appreciate it.

Francine Barbetta: Thank you for sharing with me your experience with writing a book. If my book even comes close to the beautiful writing and deeply personal touch of yours, I will consider it successful. Thank you for your help.

Heather Davulcu: My awesome cover designer. The moment I saw your artwork, I knew you were my gal! Your beautiful art was exactly what I had always imagined as the cover of my book. You're an incredible talent, and your enthusiasm and passion for the project kept me going when my energy waned. Thank you for your remarkable work and your upbeat personality and attitude. I am deeply appreciative of the art and excitement you contributed.

Paula Berinstein: My amazing editor. You have been an invaluable part of this process, and without you this book would be half the book it's become (literally and figuratively). Your patience has been beyond anything I could have imagined. Your expert knowledge, loyalty, and commitment to this project have been above and beyond all expectations. I am grateful to have found you. It was so reassuring to feel like you were sitting by my side every step of the way. Thank you for all you have done to bring this book to life and for keeping me laughing throughout the process.

My amazing test readers: Larry Necowitz, Jerry Manas, Amy Valerio, Mira Colflesh, and Jill Hammer. Thank you for taking the time out of your busy lives to test read my book. Your feedback was invaluable. Thanks so much!

My dear clients: I have learned so much from each and every one of you. You touch my heart with every story and every courageous step toward health and healing that you take. I am in awe of your bravery. I feel so honored to be invited on this journey with you. Whether you are a current or past client, came in for one session or stayed for years, you have impacted my life. You have taught me more through our relationship than I ever could have taught you. I am sure of it. I know this road we have chosen is difficult and at times lonely, but I promise you that a life of consciousness and truth-telling is worth it. I feel blessed to know you.

Table of Contents

Preface

Parenting is easy. At least I used to think so. As a psychotherapist for twenty years and a parenting skills educator for much of that time, I REALLY did think so. I used to give brilliant talks. They were true genius—engaging, inspiring, educational, and fun. After I delivered them, I would receive glowing feedback that only further validated how effective I already knew I was—until the sobering moment when someone would approach me and say, "Great talk! I learned a lot. Really funny!" And then they'd lower the boom: "You don't have any kids, do you?" UGH—I would get so angry! I didn't need to have kids in order to know how to parent. I had worked with kids and their families for decades! I knew what worked and what didn't. I resented the implication and blew off the feedback. Very mature, right?

Then in 1999, I had my first child—a beautiful little girl. At last I could put my parenting skills to the test! I did—eagerly—and they worked! Arli was (and remains) a very easy child. She was warm and loving. She went along to get along. She listened. She was appreciative and grateful. What more evidence did I need? What more evidence did THEY need? I was just an amazing parent!!!

At that time—and I am not even slightly exaggerating—I truly believed that this angel of well-behaved human goodness was the direct result of my fabulous parenting. I am actually laughing as I write this now because it is so ridiculous. But back then, I believed it with every fiber of my being. I had no idea at the time that some children come this way from the "factory."

It is clear to me now that because I believed my parenting was so wonderful, and since I believed it so strongly, God thought it best to send a very different child my way. And three years later, Zoe arrived.

It was immediately obvious that Zoe was going to be a bit more challenging. I knew it when the nurses interrupted my shower two days after the Caesarian section to tell me they were leaving her in my room because her crying was disturbing other babies. "Okay," I thought to myself, "this feels different." And it was!

As a baby, Zoe was more active than Arli, but that didn't really alarm me. Arli was strangely calm. Zoe was more like her mother. Of course, I liked that! She had fire in her belly. Passion! However, as she moved from babyhood to toddler-hood, things began to shift. She was defiant, angry, and at times out of control. I used every parenting skill I knew, but to no avail. "She is only five," I would think. "What is this going to look like at fifteen?"

Zoe's behavior was frightening. She had wild tantrums, threw scissors, and made up crazy stories that she passed off as true. For example, she would sneak into our room in the middle of the night and scream in our ears while we were sound asleep because she was angry that we wouldn't let her sleep in our bed. She was the child with whom no one wanted his or her kid to play. That's how bad it got. I was scared. Scratch that: I was petrified. And I was embarrassed. My world was coming undone. My child was out of control. I couldn't help her, and I felt like a fraud. I considered leaving my career. What could I offer families with whom I was working if I didn't even know how to help my own child?

The only thing that kept me from having a nervous break-down during this time was the faith (ironically, Faith is Zoe's middle name) that in all my years as a psychotherapist, I had never run across a severely dysfunctional adult who had been raised in a family like ours. We are loving and peaceful. We care deeply for our daughter. Most psychopaths don't have that kind of family history. Realizing that helped me calm down. And lo and behold, in the process of calming down, I noticed that things were getting better. This was a light bulb moment for me.

I began to realize that *my* anxiety about Zoe's behavior was contributing to *her* acting out. This understanding gradually led me to see how my behavior and issues directly influence my children. As I tried new strategies for calming myself and giving my daughters more space, I began to see what I'd been doing wrong and what actually works, and I developed a completely new parenting philosophy. This book is based on all that I have learned since then about how our own issues affect our children's growth and maturity. I believe that understanding this connection is the key to parenting success.

Zoe is now eleven years old. She is a wildly creative, dynamic, funny, and truly joyous child. I adore her! She does great in school and has many friends. She is the life of the party and everyone loves her. She is enormous fun and a daredevil. She is always looking for a good time. She is many, many wonderful things. The one thing she is not is easy. And "that's okay," as I say in this book many times, because she didn't come here to make my life easy. She came here to be her best self, regardless of whether that is pleasing to me or anyone else. To that end, she is doing a great job. I do believe, with all of my heart, that she came here to teach and help me heal some of my leftover wounds from childhood. By triggering my issues, she is giving me a gift. The gift is the opportunity to heal myself, which I would not be likely to do unless our relationship depended on it. She is the catalyst for this book. She has taught me patience and the art of letting go. In her own way, she has taught me what's most important—to live my best life. I am not just a parent, a daughter, a friend, a sister, a wife, or a therapist. I am a human being, seeking my own way in this world. Zoe has taught me to worry less, relax more, and manage my anxiety. With her guidance, I have learned to mind my own business and to decorate my own soul rather than trying to redirect hers. For this, and so many other reasons, I am eternally grateful for her. She is a true blessing in my life.

Through parenting both of my amazing girls, I have learned that what they most need from me is to role model the life I wish for them. Let me repeat that. What my girls most need from me as a parent is to *role model the life I wish for them.* That means taking exquisite care of *me.* Instead of living my life for *them,* I live my life for *me.* My children are a huge part of my life, but they don't make up the whole of my life. This approach works! In my practice, it has become abundantly clear that the child-centered focus of the current generation's parenting style is backfiring in a very profound way. In the previous generation, there was a lot of abuse and neglect, and even more in the generation before that, so as an almost knee-jerk reaction, we have moved to the other end of the spectrum. *We are now overinvolved, overindulgent, and over-focused on our children.* They are suffocating from this excess, and so are we. Children are emerging with depression, anxiety, and rage at earlier ages and at alarming rates.

I believe with every cell in my being that this trend can stop. It MUST stop. Many parents are lost and misguided. Countless parents think this kids-first approach is loving, gentle, and good, and that this parenting style is HELPING their children. It's not. Despite a parent's best intention, this "selfless" approach will not create independent, self-confident, self-sufficient adults.

I urge you to try another way. Stay open to the suggestions presented in this book. If you find yourself rejecting them, ask yourself why. Often, we reject approaches and ways of thinking that seem hard. We make excuses and deflect. If you choose to reject the parenting style presented in this book because it simply isn't consistent with what feels true for you, then you have my blessing to reject it. However, if you find yourself dismissing these ideas and shutting down because the work feels like it will be difficult, I encourage you to dig deeper. It will be hard, but you can do this. Your kids are counting on you, and YOUR life is waiting for you. Go get it.

Introduction: My Story

My childhood wasn't easy. My parents divorced when I was eight and my brother was four. It was unusual to have divorced parents at that time (1976), but what made me stand out even more was that it was my mother, not my father, who left. My mother didn't disappear. She was around, and I saw her mostly on weekends. However, as I moved into my moody teenage phase, I was pretty angry with a mom who would choose to leave us. So I didn't see her much during those years.

My father worked as a washer repairman, and money was always tight. My mom also had a very limited income, so extras were not a part of my life. We did not go on family vacations. I did not get treats. I remember going to the movies with my father only once—it was a Popeye movie. I remember the experience so clearly because it was such a rare occurrence. We didn't have designer clothes and we rarely went out to dinner. Life was very plain. I don't remember anyone sitting down and talking me through my friendship problems or helping me manage the day-to-day feelings I experienced. Thus, I was forced to learn how to cope on my own.

Clearly, this is not an ideal way to raise children. But it was the only way to parent that my mother and father knew. How could they be expected to do it any other way if they didn't know any other way? They didn't have role models who could guide them through the process of raising children, and I doubt they gave the issue much thought. They were distracted with their own life stressors. My father was worried about putting food on the table. My mother was concerned with getting a variety of her own needs met. They were wounded, and they were just trying to survive. I get that now.

Despite my parents' unconscious and unintentional choices, two pretty awesome kids emerged, even if I do say so myself. We did not come through childhood unscathed, but by societal standards we are quite successful. We certainly have our issues. Who doesn't? But my brother and I function pretty well. We are self-sufficient, independent, self-confident, resilient, happy adults. I often wonder how that could possibly have happened with all the sadness we experienced as children. I have given this question a tremendous amount of thought, and here is what I have concluded.

My dad was a funny guy. He still is. And while we didn't have many extras, we managed and we laughed a lot. My father's lack of funds set us up to expect very little. My brother and I are the opposite of entitled children. We expect nothing, so as adults, if we get something we are eternally grateful. Because I didn't live in anything like the lap of luxury as a child, as an adult I was thrilled to purchase and decorate a very modest home in which to raise my children. Like my dad, I am very aware of how I spend my money. I love relaxing with family and friends on vacation, and I get great joy from eating and feeding my family healthy, organic foods. Therefore, most of my discretionary spending goes to provide these pleasures.

My mother, on the other hand, gave as much as she could with the little she had. Some would say she was generous, while others might call her irresponsible. I believe my mom was a bit of both. It wasn't often, but if there was something that was important to her, she found a way to earn enough to acquire it. I'm like that too.

I think I got the best and worst of both of my parents, as most of us do. I have spent a great deal of time (and therapy dollars!) sorting through my childhood feelings. These feelings have bounced around over the years—from rage, to joy, to grief, to laughter, to appreciation. I have landed at grateful.

I know that I had the exact parents and childhood I needed in order to grow emotionally and spiritually into the woman I am today. If it weren't for the choices my parents made, albeit unconsciously, I might have turned out to be a very different person. And I'm pretty proud of who I am.

However, I do realize that it could have been possible to get all the good my parents offered without the heavy baggage that came with it. And that is what this book is about. Looking back, if I'd had the power, I would have given my parents the gifts of self-care, self-love, and self-discovery. I recognize that the only negative messages my parents passed along to my brother and me resulted from their own childhood pain and subsequent unconscious parenting decisions. These messages were NOT intentional. They loved us and would not have purposely hurt us. Most parents don't intend to cause their children pain. In my twenty-five years as a psychotherapist, I have never met one who did. Those I *have* met are struggling parents who are wounded children themselves and are attempting to parent unconsciously. This is very common, but the result is chaotic and painful for everyone involved.

This book is NOT about being a perfect parent. I know I am not perfect at parenting, and I don't claim to be. But my goal is to break the cycle of pain that has haunted my family for generations. Most damage is done through unconscious parenting. I know that when I stay connected to MYSELF and I am aware of what I am doing and why, my kids benefit. In fact, all of my relationships benefit. The truth is that many of us are guilty of parenting unconsciously. But YOU are choosing a different path because you are reading this book. Something about the title grabbed you. Instinctively, deep down, you know that you must engage in self-care and heal your childhood wounds in order to be an effective parent. You know that if you could separate your anxiety from your child's, you would parent from a clearer place. You know that when you feel whole and balanced, your kids thrive.

It is my wish that by reading this book you will become alive with possibility for yourself. From that place, you will set up the ideal fertile ground to offer your kids the same. *Your* self-care is the single greatest gift you can give to your child. And it's fun too! Learning who you are, what brings you bliss, and what triggers you, sets the stage for a joyous parenting and life experience. Immersing yourself in a pool of self-care and self-discovery creates a legacy of peace, love, and healing. If you do that, your children, grandchildren, and the world will thank you.

one

Wholeness is the Key: Live YOUR Life and Make Self-Care a Priority

If there is light in the soul, there will be beauty in the person.
If there is beauty in the person, there will be harmony in the house.
If there is harmony in the house, there will be order in the nation.
If there is order in the nation, there will be peace in the world.

~ Chinese Proverb

The first step toward effective parenting is to start with the parent, not the child. After all, we're the adults. It's up to us to create a loving and warm environment in which our children can grow. Otherwise, children could just raise themselves.

Children need us to be whole, balanced, and joyous. But no one becomes whole and balanced by accident. Quite the contrary. We do so through hard, painful work—learning who we are, testing ourselves against the world, coming to terms with our strengths and vulnerabilities, and being kind to and forgiving of ourselves. We start this work early, in our own childhoods; at least we hope we do. That's part of what childhood is for: to prepare us to be independent, well-adjusted adults. But if we start late, at least we start.

What happens to the children of parents who don't do the emotional work required to heal themselves from the wounds of their childhoods? They end up having to deal with their parents' baggage instead of focusing on their own growth, as children should. But when we are whole, we begin to role model the "secret sauce" of success to our children and are far less likely to pass along our baggage. As whole parents, we don't put the burden of our happiness on our children's shoulders. Instead, we take full responsibility for our own lives and act as examples for them.

Many of us have done the work required to feel more whole, and that's wonderful. But for those of us who have not, we must get there. In order to do that, we need to struggle with our *own* issues; only having done so can we foster wholeness and joy in our children. There's no way around the work. And why would we want to avoid it? We are here on this earth to find and create our own truth and purpose. We want that for our children. And our children want that for us. So let's not disappoint them. Our children are an important part of our lives, but they are not the whole of them. This notion makes sense theoretically, but we often stop short of doing the work necessary to create wholeness for ourselves because it can be hard and painful. We don't like pain, and we don't like struggle. And we certainly don't like seeing our kids struggle. But does anyone get anywhere without the pain? Isn't overcoming obstacles what life is about?

What I know for sure is that those of us committed to raising confident, whole children have made peace with the struggle, as it is a non-negotiable part of the parenting process. Simply put, happy children come from happy parents. And happy parents don't come without work; they are the result of gargantuan efforts to manage anxiety, cultivate a willingness to look in the mirror, and confront the vulnerabilities that get in the way of our joy. It seems ironic, doesn't it, that in order to find bliss in yourself and foster it in your children, you must learn to make peace with the very idea of struggle? It's a bittersweet certainty that baffles the best of us, yet it's a basic truth.

If you are having trouble figuring out how to create joy and peace in your home, no worries. In this book you will learn how to create your own happiness so your children are free to cultivate theirs. Let's get started.

Becoming Whole: Self-care, Self-acceptance, and Balance

You may have to change a few habits to get started on your journey; for example, the way you treat yourself. Wholeness is achieved through self-care. If you are not taking care of yourself, you should start now. Start by forgiving yourself—and your children—for the many mistakes you'll make, and have made, along the way. Accept yourself and them as fully human and fallible.

You will learn as you read on that it is vital for you to separate your own anxiety from your child's. You must feel in balance to fully enjoy your children and manage the challenges they present. They can sense when you are off-balance and on edge just as you can. Being out of balance and tense is detrimental to your relationship with your children and is often the direct result of child-centered parenting. When we are off balance, we're distracted and can't experience the full joy of this parenting journey.

Three Routes to Achieving Wholeness

When I speak about becoming more whole, I am referring to three things specifically:

1. Working toward resolving your trigger issues
2. Becoming more balanced by having varied interests
3. Working to find a holistic, healthy, balanced lifestyle that nourishes mind, body, and spiritual health.

Trigger Issues

We all have triggers. For example, one of mine is that whenever anyone isn't "getting it" fast enough, I become visibly frustrated. As you can imagine, this greatly affects my parenting. If I explain something to my children and they don't get it, I am quick to lose patience. For me, losing patience doesn't involve violent episodes, but I look exasperated, feel annoyed and frustrated, and humpf around a lot. That's not good. That's not how I want my kids to experience me.

In order to identify where this tendency comes from, I have elicited the help of a trained professional to help me understand it better and attempt to defuse it. I know that when I am not making my own needs a priority, the first thing to go is my patience. This is why self-care is so critical in child-rearing. Your triggers may be different from mine, but you have them. And I can guarantee that when you are feeling out of balance and ignoring your own needs, your kids know it and are quick to trigger your vulnerabilities. When that happens, everyone suffers. We'll talk more about ways to manage your triggers later in the book.

Balance

Let's talk a bit more about balance. Wholeness involves being fully human. That means that God did not put you on this earth to parent ONLY. If that's true for you, it will be true for your children when they grow up too. Are you parenting them just so *they* can parent, and *their* kids can parent, and on and on? No. God put you on this earth to make your mark. You are here for a reason. It's your job to find it, and it's not JUST about being a parent. Perhaps parenting *well* is your motivation to become more whole. If it is, I'll take it. But regardless of your motivation, redirect your focus AWAY from your kids and onto YOU. What makes *you* happy? What brings *you* bliss? What makes you feel like *you* are contributing to the world? Do that. Show your kids THAT. That's what they need: a whole human as a parent.

No one is perfect. No one is fully and completely whole. But some of us are further along this continuum than others. In fact, I would argue that for this current generation of parents, the majority of us are not even near the middle. We are strongly skewed toward centering our whole world around our children and their immediate needs and schedules. It's crazy, and worse yet, it is setting our children up for disaster. So, rather than creating a child-centered parenting existence, why not sign up for a meditation class, or yoga, or a cruise, or learn a language, or volunteer somewhere, or learn ballet? Anything. But please get out of the house and enjoy your life.

Our kids need to see us out of our mom and dad roles. They need to see who we are as adults. Who are our friends? What are our interests and hobbies? What makes us laugh? How do we have fun? *Our children need us to role model what it's like to be a grownup, not just a parent.* Go hang out with your friends and find a hobby that makes you smile. Turn up your favorite music and dance around the house. Show them how much FUN it is to be an adult. They are watching and learning everything from us. If we only show our children the parenting side of ourselves, we are providing an unbalanced view of adulthood. So go ahead, give yourself permission to be silly, have fun, and be sure to put your silly, playful self on display for your kids.

A Life that Nourishes Mind, Body, and Spirit

Later in the book, I offer suggestions and examples on the topic of nourishing mind, body, and spirit (see Chapter 3). For now, I would like to highlight one area that I see as extremely troublesome and that scares me tremendously: nutrition. Our nutritional intake, of lack thereof, profoundly affects our whole being—mind, body, and spirit. I am confused as to why we busy ourselves with nonsense, like making sure our kids have the latest technology, but we feed ourselves and our children crap. The obesity rate has risen to out-of-control levels, and as a result our kids are the first generation that will not live as long as their parents. Does that scare anyone but me? If it scares you too, do something now: join a gym, experiment with healthy vegetarian or vegan alternatives, learn to cook, create a cook-off day with friends where you all choose a healthy recipe and spend the day together cooking for yourselves and your families. Everyone gets along better when they are properly fed. And I don't mean fed as in not hungry. I mean our body needs to take in appropriate nutrition to function properly. When we are not giving our body the nutrition it needs, our mood, behavior, and overall attitude are poor. This is a major issue in families today, yet it is the last thing parents look to as the problem. Way too many parents are far more likely to put their children on medication than they are to change their diet. I think that's a huge mistake.

Put Yourself First

Remember, we are going to role model the life we wish for our children, and in order to do that, our needs as parents and caregivers must be met BEFORE our children's needs. We can't role model by obsessing over them. We have to let go and allow their lives to be a separate, albeit important, part of ours. Give your children the gift of a cheerful, balanced parent and you have cracked the code for raising joyous children.

When our children become the center of our universe, we inappropriately place the burden of responsibility on them to make us happy. That is very unfair and rarely goes well. If they have a good day, we do too. If they have a bad day, we do too. If they have a fight with their friends, we're miserable right along with them. If they get a bad grade, we're the ones who are upset. That's way too much pressure to put on a child. And it's exhausting for everyone.

Make your *own* life the priority. Decorate your own soul and let your children be an important part of the life you create for yourself. When you focus on your own fulfillment, your children have freedom to grow, explore, and make mistakes without the added burden of worrying about how you will be affected and how you will react.

Your Child's Life is Not Your Life

We need to refocus. Take grades, for example. Many parents focus their attention on helping their children achieve great grades. Instead, why don't we place more emphasis on encouraging greatness as *human beings?* Your child will feel more whole when you do, and the world will become a much happier, more peaceful place! How is this done? It's done by children watching parents, of course.

What behaviors do you model that make you a great human? I recommend starting by demonstrating self-management and self-care. Put simply, self-management and self-care are the greatest gifts you can give to your children. SHOW them, don't TELL them, how to live a life of joy, balance, limits, and discipline. Showing them how it's done is your job. Your children add joy and color and love to your life, and you learn lessons from them, but it is *not* their job to give you a reason to wake up in the morning. Giving them so much power to make you happy and fulfilled is far too heavy a burden to place on the vulnerable shoulders of a child. Create a vibrant, meaningful life for yourself with space for your children to watch you thrive. Enjoy your children in a way that adds to an already beautiful and deeply rich life. By doing so, you are giving your children a gift that will have a profound impact: a parent who is whole and healed. Children mimic what they see. Be a whole, healed self, and that's what your children will emulate.

The possibilities for creating "wholeness" in your life are endless, and the only limitations are those created in your own mind. My most favorite self-care activities are meditation and cooking healthy vegan food. I find that when I make time for both of these activities, my whole being shifts into a place of calm and peace. It affects me emotionally, physically and spiritually in a profound way.

Becoming more whole may look very different for you. Maybe you need more alone time, or more time with friends. Maybe you need to take a vacation or a long, hot bubble bath. Here's a challenge for you: stop reading and go to your calendar right now and find three open dates. Fill them in with things that you will do that are just for you. They cannot involve your children—just you, or maybe you and a friend, or you and your partner. Write in what you will do that day and follow through—even if it's as simple as taking a bath.

I encourage you to pay very close attention to your mood that day and how you interact with your children. Are you more patient? More engaged? More interested? After you have spent time doing what you want to do, stay conscious of your interactions with your children in the days that follow. How have your perceptions shifted, if at all? Write them down and review them often. Once you see proof that self-care is a vital component in your children's healthy upbringing and a key ingredient in strengthening your relationship with them, you will make time for it and do it over and over again. But don't take my word for it; experiment with it yourself. See if it is as worthwhile and as powerful as I say it is. I'll bet you will be blown away by the results!

Chapter One Take-away

Children need us to be whole, balanced, and joyous. We must struggle with our own issues in order to get there. Struggle can be painful and difficult, but it's the only way to become more whole. When we role model what happy, balanced adults are like, our children will emulate us and become whole human beings themselves.

two

Create a Family Hierarchy That Lets Kids Thrive

A family in harmony will prosper in everything.
~ Chinese Proverb

Our children actually require very little. They need the simple things in life, such as love, a peaceful household, parents who can work together to guide them (regardless of whether they are married, divorced, or never married), and limits. They need you to have reasonable expectations of them and communicate those expectations clearly. They need to feel safe so they can take the necessary risks inherent in growing up. They need NOT to feel afraid of you. They need to respect you. And most important, they need not have to shoulder your burdens on top of their own. If you work toward wholeness, they won't have to.

Above all else, children need love, guidance, nurturing, and boundaries. For that to happen, they need to be placed appropriately in the family hierarchy—beneath, not above us. This placement makes them feel safe. They need us to set rules and limits for them. They need consequences—not punishment—for rule infractions. They need us to respond to these infractions with kindness and love, but also consistent follow-through with appropriate consequences. Our children want and need for us to encourage, but not demand, positive behaviors from them. They need us to back off, let go, and allow them to experience the natural and logical consequences that result from learning how the world works. We need to let them take responsibility for their successes and their failures as we encourage them to try again and again. If we can manage our anxiety over their actions and choices and empower our children to take responsibility for their lives, we will set the groundwork for an amazing parenting journey. This poem by Kahlil Gibran illustrates these points beautifully.

On Children

Your children are not your children.
They are the sons and daughters of Life's longing for itself.
They come through you but not from you,
And though they are with you, yet they belong not to you.

You may give them your love but not your thoughts.
For they have their own thoughts.
You may house their bodies but not their souls,
For their souls dwell in the house of tomorrow, which you cannot visit, not even in your dreams.
You may strive to be like them, but seek not to make them like you.
For life goes not backward nor tarries with yesterday.

You are the bows from which your children as living arrows are sent forth.
The archer sees the mark upon the path of the infinite, and He bends you with His might that His arrows may go swift and far.
Let your bending in the archer's hand be for gladness;
For even as He loves the arrow that flies, so He loves also the bow that is stable.

Raising Whole Children

When you create a healthy family hierarchy, you set up an environment in which children thrive. The optimal structure puts you at the top, then your partner relationship (e.g., spouse, co-parent), with your children at the bottom.

Children will feed from this flow; they will have the freedom to move through childhood without having to be the center of attention all the time. However, many people have this structure reversed so the children are at the top, then the partner, with the parent at the bottom.

By putting children at the top of the hierarchy, we create a dynamic that is unhealthy and unbalanced. Aren't we supposed to put our child's needs before our own? No! Staying balanced and keeping yourself as the priority, then your partner relationship, then your children, is the key to raising children who will become self-sufficient, kind, independent adults.

Putting children at the bottom of the family hierarchy is rare in this generation. Because we grew up in an era when children were often expected to be seen and not heard, we have overreacted to our early experiences and swung to the other side of the continuum. In so doing, we have managed to set our kids up for hardship, just as many of our parents did when they ignored us or noticed us just to impose discipline. Need more convincing? Here are some points to consider.

1. **Kids at the top think they're in charge.** You may be asking yourself, "What could possibly be wrong with putting our children first?" The simple answer is "Everything!" When you place your children at the top of the family

hierarchy, you are sending them a clear message: "In this family, you are in charge." If you do that, prepare yourself for the consequences of a child-centered home. Putting children at the top of the hierarchy, regardless of age, has devastating consequences, both to their own development and the family system overall. Imagine what a family looks like with a four-year-old in charge. A ten-year-old. A teenager. It's scary. Most parents don't realize that placing their child's needs ahead of their own sets up this "you-are-in-charge" dynamic, but it does. And since parents don't realize what's happening, they are terribly befuddled when things begin to go wrong.

Some parents worry that changing the hierarchy means that they can no longer help guide their children. I assure you, it means nothing of the kind. Of course you can still help guide them. In fact, I believe you can guide them better if *you're* at the top because that way, they will look up to you. Whoever is at the top is the one with the responsibility to lead. If they are at the top, shouldn't they be guiding you?

2. **Kids at the top don't feel safe.** Children need to feel safe in order to thrive. When children are placed at the top of the family system, they feel quite unsafe. They feel unsafe because at a core, instinctive level, they know they don't belong there. They know they are new on this planet and they need guidance and authority to help them. What they want is to have a loving, consistent, clear authority figure shine the light and create boundaries so they can find their way.

3. **Parents can't communicate their expectations and foster respect from the bottom of the hierarchy.** When children are placed at the top of the hierarchy, they call the shots. That means you're essentially at their beck and call. However, when you place children in the *appropriate* position in the family hierarchy, you set up a structure in which expectations can be clearly communicated and known. This structure is the groundwork for a healthy parent/child relationship. It is the foundation for a relationship in which respect and love flow both ways, allowing children to choose the life *they* want to live. This includes experiencing consequences for poor choices that are "okay" and accepted as part of growing up. When children make mistakes within the hierarchy, consequences are swift, clear, calm, and loving. And because there is an expectation that they are children *learning* about the world, there is no anger or disappointment needed to drive the point home. Learning means making mistakes. They don't need to be berated or lectured to or belittled. A simple consequence will do; that's how they'll learn that certain actions lead to certain results. This hierarchy sets your home up as a loving, living lab of learning, in which children can experiment and see what happens. The hierarchy and the subsequent behaviors that flow from it set your child up for a life of peace, respect, and love. It's nearly impossible for a child to learn respect when she starts out in charge.

Many families that adopt a kids-first philosophy wind up in my office. In my practice, I work almost exclusively with parents. I rarely find it necessary to meet directly with a child. It is the parents who have set up this dynamic, and it is the parents who need to reconstruct it, placing themselves back at the top. This approach is a hard sell when I meet with parents alone, but nearly impossible if children are in the room. In fact, having the child in the room sends the message that she has a say in what happens next, when in fact, she doesn't—at least not on my watch. As you might imagine, this is not a popular therapeutic style with many parents, despite the fact that it works.

What I typically find is that there are two types of parents who come to see me. There are the courageous, evolved parents who make an appointment early in the parenting journey, when they first become aware that issues are brewing. However, more often, I am called out of a desperate need, when parents are in despair and have tried a more traditional, "safer" family therapy approach that has failed. It's threatening to look at your own parenting style as the first line of defense when things start moving in an uncomfortable direction, and not everyone can do it.

However, if you can develop the courage and *willingness* to put yourself first, you will be well positioned to live a peaceful life and increase your chances of avoiding the kinds of problems experienced by the following families. (Names and details have been changed for purposes of confidentiality).

Family Stories

Mark: Four Years Old

Mark's parents believed that a child-centered family was the key to raising a successful, well-adjusted child. As is often the case, both parents had experienced traumatic childhoods. They described feeling unheard, invisible, and unloved. Mom characterized her parents as alcoholic, and felt unnoticed most of her childhood. Her parents were preoccupied with getting their next drink, not parenting. Since Mom felt so wounded as a result of her parents' drinking and their subsequent neglect, she wanted to be sure to give Mark lots of attention. Dad described his father as absent and his mother as depressed. He and his five siblings received very little attention. Dad would often describe his childhood as having been devoid of love. He stated that he felt he had to raise himself in many ways. Clearly, he didn't want that for his own children.

Once you understand the trauma Mark's parents endured, you can see how they wished for a different experience for their own child. So once Mark arrived, it was all Mark, all the time. If Mark wanted to be held, he was held. If Mark wanted chicken nuggets for dinner, chicken nuggets it was. If Mark didn't want to drink water, he got juice. If he didn't want juice, he got soda. If Mark didn't want Mommy and Daddy to go out, he screamed until they relented and stayed home. By four years old, he had received the message loud and clear: "I am the all-important and powerful Mark. Life revolves around me. My needs are all that matter here."

Mark wasn't potty trained because he preferred to use a pull-up. The potty training failure and the embarrassment that resulted are what finally motivated his parents to come see me. What amazed me was not that there was a four-year-old who wasn't potty trained. What shocked me was how his parents couldn't see their part in the problem and weren't alarmed about Mark's other concerning behaviors. In fact, they were fine with how over-attached he was. They thought it was cute. It made them feel loved and connected, which validated for them that they were great parents. It was clear I had my work cut out for me!

First, I focused on the presenting problem—the potty training—as this was their primary concern. So I went to work teaching them how to potty train their child. Potty training a child who has received the message that he is in charge isn't easy. It requires reversing the message. The message needs to go from "Pee and poop in your diaper anytime you feel the need *and I will take care of it for you*" to "Pee and poop in your diaper anytime you feel the need *and you will need to take care of it yourself.*"

The complicating issue was that reversing the message would require Mark to be unhappy and uncomfortable for a while, and therefore so would his parents. His parents couldn't tolerate that. Because of their own unprocessed childhood trauma, they found it near torture to allow their child to "suffer," because seeing Mark "suffer" unconsciously reminded them of their own childhood hurts. I tried to help them separate these issues, as Mark was not truly suffering; he was simply struggling through a normal developmental stage. But watching Mark struggle triggered their own childhood distress; his struggle and their pain were linked in their minds. This is why it is CRITICAL that parents work to heal themselves so they do not confuse their child's challenges with their own.

Without self-awareness, parents risk being incapable of giving their children what they need. Children need you to see them for who *they* are and what *they* need. They are not a reflection of your own childhood and what *you* needed. In addition to love, children also need structure, discipline, and limits. They need you to parent consciously, not reactively. Parenting in *reaction* to the parenting (or lack thereof) you received is as dysfunctional as parenting the same way you were parented. Most parents don't realize that. They think they are doing a great job by doing the opposite of what their parents did. Parents are aware that they didn't get their own needs met as kids, so they assume if they do the opposite, their kids will get what they need. That's simply not true. In fact, I believe this parenting style is quite dangerous.

It is critical that you parent from a place of consciousness. Be clear about what you want to do with parenting and how you want to do it. You don't need to parent perfectly. That is not even close to what is required. Children recover quite nicely from poor parenting choices that are made from a conscious place. Good parenting requires that you parent thoughtfully and deliberately. From there, feel free to be as imperfect as possible! We are human. We won't make every decision correctly. But choose your approaches with conscious awareness.

Parents often think they are parenting consciously, but really they are just reacting in a knee-jerk fashion. It is in that knee-jerk parenting that we get into trouble. This is how our kids become wounded. In many cases parents are hurting their children emotionally while simultaneously feeling one hundred percent confident that they are helping them reach their greatest potential. It's a bitter irony I see every day in my practice.

I told Mark's parents that unless they were able to accept the importance of working on healing their own childhood traumas, Mark had little chance of learning how to navigate the world on his own, and that he might never learn that he is capable of managing without them. Unfortunately, Mark's parents were unable to do the work and left therapy after a short while. The idea of looking at their own issues was too much for them to handle, as it is for many parents. It was just too scary. To truly help Mark, his parents would need to walk through the fire of their own pain and history. They wanted to avoid that, although they weren't even conscious of this avoidance. When I gently confronted them with my assessment, that they were avoiding the pain of their own childhood at Mark's expense, they dismissed me. They felt strongly, as many parents do, that they could bypass their own work and focus solely on the presenting problem of their child. They insisted on finding a therapist who would see Mark as the problem and help him learn to use the toilet without any discomfort to him. I wished them luck with that.

If they had been willing to do the work, they would have discovered that a consciousness follows that allows parents to begin to separate their experiences from their child's. Mark's parents couldn't allow him to be uncomfortable because they had spent a lifetime avoiding being uncomfortable themselves. You can't take your children any further than you have travelled. This truth, and many people's unwillingness to do their own work, feels tragic to me, mostly because the pain this parenting style can cause is unnecessary and avoidable. I wish I could fast-forward the clock and show parents what is coming down the road if they don't shift the focus off of their child and onto themselves. Parents must find a way to work through these personal issues with the loving guidance of a compassionate, skilled therapist. If they don't, the consequences will be profound for all.

Unfortunately, I see the result of this parenting style every day, and it is one of the reasons I wrote this book. I have clients whose teenage children still wet the bed; they often see this as the children's immaturity or willful attempt to remain irresponsible and defiant. Many parents go through rounds of biological testing to see why their children can't hold their urine until the morning. However, the vast majority of these cases are the direct result of parents' unresolved issues or lack of parenting skills to which the children are unconsciously reacting. The parents' leftover pain from a childhood riddled with abuse and neglect is driving their decisions, when what should be guiding them is the children's actual needs. As a result, with their needs unmet, these children will unconsciously act out in rage or depression. These difficulties, and many others, can be avoided by putting your own needs, your own healing, and your own life at the top of the hierarchy.

Suzy: Ten Years Old

Suzy's family came to see me because at the young age of ten, she was already expressing feelings of self-hatred and had even, on occasion, threatened to kill herself. As you can imagine, her parents were devastated and bewildered. They had always given Suzy everything she wanted and had provided her with a charmed life. She had many toys and gadgets. She had travelled the world, often missing school to fly off to Japan, Europe, or Disney World. Suzy knew no limits. What reason would she have to be depressed? She had EVERYTHING a girl could want. In addition to many material possessions, she had the unrelenting commitment of and attention from her parents. Suzy was their pride and joy! She was a delight. They prided themselves on Suzy's ability to behave in expensive restaurants and speak intelligently about her world travels to her peers. She was a parent's dream.

When Suzy began to express feelings of low self-esteem, they called a psychiatrist, who immediately prescribed medication that didn't seem to help. Soon, Suzy refused therapy and medication, and her symptoms became more exaggerated. It was out of desperation that her mom and dad agreed to see me. Suzy's parents were refreshingly open and willing to change their approach. Suzy was one lucky young lady! Many parents aren't nearly as flexible as hers were. They began to look at the issues that had set up this parenting style in the first place. Some of them stemmed from a marriage that was not getting enough attention. Through the process of psychotherapy, Mom and Dad realized that, and that their childhood experiences of deprivation and boredom had unconsciously triggered a desire to fill their own voids by providing extravagances to Suzy. *You CANNOT heal your childhood wounds vicariously through your children—by giving them what you perceive was lacking in your own experience.* This approach will backfire every time. In Suzy's case (as in the case of almost all children), all she wanted and needed were love, limits, peace, and simple living. Simple living can include, but is not limited to, not being pulled out of school regularly for vacations, parents who like each other and get along, friends to play with in the backyard, healthy meals eaten together, conversation, and a genuine interest in her life while you go about living your own. That's it. But Suzy was too busy for the simple things. She didn't require fancy clothes, extravagant vacations, electronic gadgets, or a thousand toys. She needed simplicity. She craved peace as we all do.

Suzy's parents were willing to try some new approaches. I worked with them to experiment by removing the extravagances one at a time to see what was complicating, or perhaps creating, Suzy's feeling of being overwhelmed. Suzy's mom and dad were more than willing to entertain the idea that their parenting style wasn't consistent with their daughter's needs. This is critical. That *willingness* ("willingness" is my favorite word) is what sets Suzy's parents apart from many who fail. Parents who come to see a therapist all want their family circumstances to improve, but they are not always willing to do the personal work to make that happen. We WANT something different, but few are WILLING to DO something different. Suzy was one of the lucky ones. Her parents were WILLING. Again, parents are not lacking in good intentions, but effective parenting requires more than that. It's not enough to love our children, and it's not enough to want the best for them. We also need to be willing to stretch ourselves beyond what *should* work and try something that *will* work, and not give up until a solution is found.

As her parents began to simplify Suzy's life and focus more on their own, Suzy's depression lifted quickly. What is so interesting to me is that as is the case for many families I see, as Suzy's parents shifted their focus back to their own needs and their marriage, Suzy didn't even question what they were doing. This phenomenon is similar to what happens when we are well: we don't notice how we feel until we get sick and are miserable. Suzy's family was essentially sick when the spotlight was on her, but when they got well, no one batted an eye. Suzy (and the whole family) simply started to heal. Her parents were delighted and relieved to learn that they DID have the ability to influence Suzy's depression. In my experience, although there is a biological component to childhood depression, there is almost always a trigger or an environmental stressor in play. And while effective parenting may not be the complete solution, it has great influence. We are far more powerful than we think.

Johnny: Fifteen Years Old

As is typically the case when I receive a call from a parent of an adolescent, Johnny was already out of control. For many families, crisis must hit before they are *willing* to come for parenting coaching sessions. The trend is to send kids, not parents, to therapy when problems arise. It is only in desperate times and after many failed send-the-kid-to-therapy treatment attempts that parents are finally willing to look at themselves.

Johnny was rude, disrespectful, and oppositional. He often cursed at his parents, refused to honor the curfew they set for him, and had recently started to use drugs. His parents were frantic. Johnny had always been a "good kid," whatever that means. In this case, I believe they were referring to his good grades in elementary school and his easygoing demeanor throughout his younger years. His recent behavior had seemed to present itself out of the blue once Johnny started middle school.

As I started to take a family history and learned their parenting style, I discovered that Mom and Dad rarely set limits with Johnny. "We didn't need to!" they protested. "He was a great kid." I learned that Johnny could eat what he wanted when he wanted, do what he wanted when he wanted, talk however he wanted when he wanted, and so on. When he would break the occasional family rule, there were never any consequences. And in the rare circumstance in which the parents did try to institute a consequence, there was never any follow-through.

This worked okay (so his parents said) until adolescence, when the road got bumpy. Suddenly, rules and limits were flying up all over the place out of necessity and Johnny would have none of them. He laughed in his parents' faces as if to say "Rules? Are you kidding me? I never had any rules before, and I never had any consequences either." Kids know instinctively that if there haven't been any consequences for small missteps, it's because you are terrible at following through. So although they have always been in the driver's seat, once adolescence hits, they take full advantage and the situation quickly begins to spin out of control. I am always curious when I meet parents who set few or no limits with their young children and then seem surprised when things fall apart in adolescence. It is necessary to teach children from a young age who is in charge. We teach them that we are in charge when we are kind, firm, set limits, and follow through with consequences when rules are broken. If you haven't set up this structure in your family, you can't blame your children when they start to act like they own the place. If they are behaving in a way that is wildly inappropriate and disrespectful, you can bet that they have always gotten the message that they could do what they wanted and that their needs were top priority. This reaction is another result of a child-centered approach to parenting.

I began to work with Johnny's parents to help them learn how to set limits with him. Through this process I learned that Mom had been physically abused as a child. If she stepped out of line, she was smacked. Dad's family history was quite similar. Both grew up afraid of their parents, and that was the last thing they wanted Johnny to feel about them. In reaction to their own childhood experiences, they had unconsciously set themselves up for the situation they now found themselves in with Johnny. Resisting—or refusing—to look at your own issues sets you and your children up for struggle throughout your parenting journey. Johnny's parents really struggled to set limits with him, and he continued to spiral out of control.

Eventually, I was able to convince each of them to work on their own childhood traumas to clear the way to parent more effectively. As they looked more closely at their own pain and family-of-origin histories, it became clear to them that their fears of abuse would not be realized by simply setting limits and following through with consequences. Abuse and limits are very different concepts. In fact, they are polar opposites. Setting limits with our children is a loving gesture that they desperately crave. Abuse (physical intimidation or infliction of pain) is an unloving, reactive, acting out behavior that parents use when they have lost control of themselves and are parenting unconsciously. Physical intimidation and emotional abuse *are not* parenting strategies; they are the exact opposite. Setting limits with love *is* a critical parenting skill. And it works because it keeps children at the appropriate spot in the hierarchy and helps them to feel safe.

Johnny's parents and I continued to work together until they could differentiate between these two concepts (limits vs. abuse). Although it took time, both parents were eventually able to set limits with Johnny, and he responded favorably. Johnny started to experience consequences for his disrespectful behavior. If he behaved inappropriately, a consequence followed quickly. As his parents became more practiced at setting limits and following through with consequences *every time Johnny acted out,* Johnny's behavior started to fall in line. For example, if he came in past his curfew, the consequence was that he couldn't go out the following day. If he spoke disrespectfully to his mom on his way out the door to baseball practice, Mom refused to drive him. If he angrily announced that he hated Mom's cooking, Mom stopped cooking for him. If he refused to go to school, rather than getting into a verbal altercation with him, his parents simply called the truancy officer to escort him to school.

As this regimen became the norm, Johnny got the message that he was no longer in charge. As I say in Chapter 5, it's never too early or too late to make changes in your parenting approach. If your way of doing things isn't working, regardless of your child's age, stop and find another. You can't control what your children ultimately decide as their life path, but you can decide at any time whether to be part of the solution or part of the problem. Johnny's parents were successful at being part of the solution primarily because they were *willing* to take the focus off Johnny and his acting out behaviors and place the spotlight on themselves. In my experience, refocusing in this way is a parent's greatest chance at profoundly influencing a child's life in a positive, healthy way.

Julia: Eighteen Years Old

Julia was an only child whose parents came to me after trying every form of therapy, private school, alternative school, and medication available. They were at their wits' end. As an only child, Julia received lots of attention from her parents. She was a beautiful, smart, mature, talented artist. Her parents were successful, educated, attractive, loving people. They were happily married, and while no marriage is perfect, they were fairly aligned in their parenting style. Dad had the occasional angry outburst and Mom experienced the periodic depressive episode, but the one thing they could wholeheartedly rejoice in was the joy their child brought them.

As is so often the case in one-child families, Julia was everything to them. Parents of only children need to work overtime to avoid creating a child-centered world because it is set up that way by default. At least in families with multiple children, attention must be spread around because the other kids demand it. In the case of an only child, there are few distractions. It is possible to raise a well-adjusted only child, but it requires conscious, evolved parents who have a full and complete life separate from their child. I find that in the case of parents of only children, this is rarely the case. More typically, only-child families are set up with the world revolving around the child.

Like many only children, Julia was worshipped by her parents. The sun rose and set on her. This may sound like a dream to those of us who didn't get enough attention as kids, but let me assure you, it is a nightmare scenario. It didn't take long for Julia to feel the heavy burden that comes with being responsible for your parents' happiness. My most challenging cases are the ones like Julia who are only children, or those where parents have unconsciously laid the burden of their fulfillment in life squarely on their child's shoulders. They don't realize it, of course, but the lifelong message sent is "Please be good, polite, successful, and beautiful, and make us look good, no matter the cost to your own needs." It's true. And it's ugly. And worse, parents have no conscious awareness that it is happening. Again, here we have a family who is role modeling the exact opposite of self-care. The message the parents are sending and Julia is receiving is "Take care of my needs, not your own. We brought you into this world so you could take care of us and make us feel good and whole. Now get to work!"

I worked with this family for many years. Initially, both Julia and her parents struggled. She started to use drugs (heroin was her drug of choice), and she became more and more distant from the family that she felt was suffocating her. However, over the years, through gaining awareness of their choices, Julia's parents did an outstanding job of changing their approach. They got to work looking at the issues that kept them from having a life separate from their daughter. Through psychotherapy, they became conscious of the ways in which they were unknowingly placing the burden of responsibility for their moods, happiness, and life fulfillment on Julia's shoulders. Once they reached this understanding, since Julia was already eighteen and they felt their time to change things was rapidly dissipating, they got to work quickly. They started to go on date nights and even travelled without her. They started paying much less attention to Julia and much more attention to themselves, both individually and as a couple. This wasn't easy for them, but they became convinced that their way hadn't worked. They were *willing* to try something new and the shift was almost immediate. Julia took notice, and things began to improve quickly. Within a year, Julia got sober, went to college, and started to have a real chance at a joyous, fulfilling life. Everyone, including me, began to breathe a sigh of relief. It looked like Julia was on the path toward recovery. Her parents eventually discontinued therapy with my blessing.

Several years later I learned that Julia had died from an accidental heroin overdose. It was quite a shock to us all. When I attended her funeral, I learned that Julia had in fact remained sober in the years since we had completed therapy. Unfortunately however, the memory of the heroin high haunted her as it does many recovering addicts. I don't believe Julia's parents could have prevented her choice to get high "one last time," as her diary stated. That was Julia's choice. Her parents did everything in their power to get themselves well as quickly as they could so they could parent Julia in the way she needed. For Julia, however, it was too late.

When I think about this case and feel the pain and sadness of its outcome, I am reminded of something I heard leadership guru John Maxwell say at a conference I attended recently. He suggests that it's not the fastest person who wins the race, but rather the one who starts the soonest. I often wonder if Julia's tragic death could have been averted had her parents started the race to get themselves well sooner. I'm not sure. But I think we tip the odds in our favor when we start earlier on this path of self-care. Just as I don't believe my decision to be a vegan will eliminate my chances of developing cancer, I know from the research I've done that I have greatly reduced the odds of that happening. I don't know if Julia's life could have been saved, but perhaps if her parents had become aware of the need for self-care as their priority sooner, things might have ended differently.

If you can truly take the message of this book in and assimilate it into your being, I believe you can greatly reduce the chances of a tragic circumstance such as Julia's in your family. It is crucial for your child's development that you make yourself, your needs, your healing, and your life the priority. I know Julia's parents would agree. They told me that while it was too late for Julia, their hope and prayer was that other families would get the message sooner, and that perhaps their story might help prevent a similar outcome for others. My wish for you is the same as Julia's parents': get started on this self-care journey sooner rather than later. Parenting is a joyous, beautiful experience that need not be fraught with endless struggle and immense sacrifice. I hope that by the end of our experience together, I have convinced you to abandon the sacrifice and martyrdom and go get yourself a LIFE! And it would really help your kids if you enjoy it while you're at it.

Risa: Sixteen Years Old

I never met Risa. As with many of my clients, meeting the "problem child" is rarely necessary since it is the parenting style that typically needs to change to make a significant, positive impact in the family system. When Risa's mom came to see me she was quite distressed. She was riddled with worry and fear for Risa. As I inquired further, Risa's mom described her as a "pathological procrastinator." The problem was that Risa would wait until the last minute to complete important school assignments and then panic the night before because the assignment was not finished. Risa's mom worked tirelessly with her to create the skills to stop the cycle of procrastination, then panic, then dread, then the meltdown that would lead her to avoid school that day.

Risa's parents often sat down with her to develop a plan that never worked. This created more struggle, tension, and anger in all members of the family. Risa and her parents would usually end these episodes in conflict and anger. I asked her mom why she felt it was her responsibility to come up with a plan to enable Risa to remember to do her own homework assignment. She thought for a moment and then replied, "Because she's my daughter; that's my job." Our work started right there because I completely disagreed with her. It is not "our job" to fix every issue in our child's life. We have a job, but that's not it. It is our job to create consequences if there aren't natural and logical ones built into the situation. But more than that, it is DEFINITELY our job to manage our anxiety about our kids' choices so they can develop the skills required for life.

Mom thought I would be helping her come up with strategies to help Risa procrastinate less. Instead, I worked with Risa's mom to uncover why she felt responsible for Risa's homework and skill deficit. Risa had not asked for help with her procrastination. Mom assumed she wanted help because she was struggling. This is a mistake parents often make. We see a problem, so we think we must fix it. Not so. Fixing it feels like the easier path when compared with the more effective alternative, which is to manage our own anxiety so our children can figure it out for themselves.

In Risa's case, her mom spent several years in therapy working on her own anxiety, its cause, and the triggers that increased her anxiety when Risa didn't react as SHE would in a similar situation. As Mom got clearer about whose issue it was, she started to back off and let Risa *struggle*. At first, Risa was angry and expressed feeling lost and abandoned. But as her mom gained confidence that letting Risa figure out what to do on her own was in her best interest, things began to settle. This is not to say that Risa miraculously stopped procrastinating. In fact, the situation got worse before it got better. This created an opportunity for Mom to get lots of practice in self-care and anxiety management.

Within a year, Risa, now a senior in high school, realized that no one was suffering by her procrastination but her. She started to develop her own coping skills and strategies to avoid procrastinating. She started to feel confident and in charge of her vulnerabilities. She started to realize that although her tendency to procrastinate was a struggle for her, she was able to manage it in a way that worked. Risa's self-confidence increased significantly, and her mom was overjoyed, proud, and amazed.

Risa's mom recently had to say goodbye to her as she left for college. There were many tears shed, but mostly tears of joy as they all felt grateful for what they had accomplished. Saying goodbye to your child as she leaves for college is always bittersweet, but for Risa's mom, it was far more sweet than bitter, as she felt that through her self-care approach and anxiety management, she was able to create an environment in which Risa could thrive.

I have worked with hundreds of families over the years, and there is one thing that I know is true. Parents who can internalize and behave out of a place of self-care in child-rearing enjoy the parenting journey far more than those who take on the child-centered, martyred approach. The children fare far better and emerge as adults with less anxiety, more joy, and a solid relationship with their parents. A relationship emerges that is based on love and respect rather than anger and resentment. These kids are happier, more responsible, and emotionally free. I have had the pleasure of working with many families who have changed their approach midway through the child-rearing journey, and some who have changed direction at the eleventh hour, literally, in the senior year of high school. Regardless of when you get the message, a noticeable, positive shift away from a child-centered approach creates a new joy. This self-care approach will bring you newfound pleasure in parenting you never thought possible. My suggestion: do it. Take the plunge. Dive into your life and trust that ironically, focusing on your own joy is what your child needed from you all along.

Chapter Two Take-away

When children are placed under the parents in the family hierarchy, they are set up for success. When they're placed at the top, they feel vulnerable and weighed down, and they can't become whole, well-adjusted adults. If your hierarchy is upside down, correct it now.

three
Managing Parental Anxiety

The truth is that our finest moments are most likely to occur when we are feeling deeply uncomfortable, unhappy, or unfulfilled. For it is only in such moments, propelled by our discomfort, that we are likely to step out of our ruts and start searching for different ways or truer answers.

~ *M. Scott Peck*

On behalf of your children, I want to thank you. You are giving them an amazing gift. They are truly lucky to have you as a parent. I mean that. Since you are still reading this book, I trust that you care enough to try to manage your own anxiety. Maybe you want a different childhood for your kids than you had. Maybe you want to bring your family back into balance because you are not satisfied with the way your parenting is going at present.

Managing our anxiety is required if we are to let our children struggle through their various stages. Letting them struggle is necessary for their emotional and spiritual maturity. Children (or any human or animal) cannot learn in an anxious environment. When anxiety is high, nothing can be communicated or taught. When anxiety is low, the possibilities for communication and learning are limitless. When we are reacting to our children in an angry, frustrated, or disappointed manner, anxiety is high.

It's a lot like talking to an alcoholic about his drinking when he is intoxicated (yup, I've made that mistake). It's totally pointless. You might as well bang your head against a brick wall. If you want to be heard, if you really want things to change, wait until you (and the child) are calm enough to have a discussion. This takes great patience and self-control. If you can manage it, you will be blown away by the results!

How can we manage our own anxiety so that we can parent more effectively? Here are a few strategies I've learned along the way.

Breathe In, Breathe Out

Toddlers have tantrums. Siblings argue. Children break the rules. Parents don't always agree on parenting styles. It's all okay. These are not our biggest problems. Our reaction to them is a far more important issue. Stop focusing on the question "How do I handle it when my child/partner/kids_____?" Instead, focus on yourself and your internal reaction.

If your child is having a tantrum in the car, breathe. If your partner disagrees with you, breathe. If your kids are arguing with each other, breathe. After you have calmed yourself down by taking several long, deep breaths, the how-to-do-it of a situation will come to you in an easier, gentler, clearer way. You have all the answers within you; getting to them is just a matter of accessing your intuition. Doing that in an anxious state is impossible.

Managing Anxiety Through Meditation

Breathe in. Hold it. Keep holding it. Breathe out verrrrrrry slowly. Repeat. Repeat again. Ahhhh, meditation! I believe meditation is AS powerful if not MORE so than any anti-anxiety medication. But please, consult your physician prior to changing or stopping medication. Both can be very useful. How strange it is that meditation and medication are almost the same word. Coincidence? But I digress.

If you can learn to observe your own emotions rather than exploding outward, you will master the art of self-management. Once self-management is mastered, your world expands to one of limitless possibilities. When your children don't have to worry about you and your reactions, they are free to be the kids they were born to be. And you get to be their biggest cheerleader and coach, supporting them every step of the way. I encourage you to seek out a meditation class in your area. It will help you enjoy the experience of parenting rather than being stressed by it. Your home will become a place of peace, love, and serenity. And the whole world will too.

Don't Forget to Laugh

Never lose your sense of humor (and if you don't have one, find the funniest person you know and sign up for funny camp!). It is a game-changing parenting skill. How wonderful it is to give your child the gift of seeing that life's ups and downs are just so funny. Wouldn't it be great if he knew that what he is going through is just a little blip on the screen; that depending on the infraction, it probably won't matter in ten minutes, ten hours, or ten years? Remember when we were in high school and we were told, "If you do that again, it's going on your permanent record"? What permanent record? There is no such thing. Every single thing is temporary. Even life itself is temporary. So the best way to move through a difficult stage with your child is to pay as little attention to it as possible. That doesn't mean you accept unacceptable behavior. It simply means you hand out an appropriate, logical consequence with very little pomp and circumstance and then find a friend or significant other to laugh with so that you don't take the misbehavior too seriously.

Have Compassion—Forgive Yourself

Ralph Waldo Emerson was a smart guy. One of the things he said was this: "Finish each day and be done with it. You have done what you could. Some blunders and absurdities no doubt crept in; forget them as soon as you can. Tomorrow is a new day. You shall begin it serenely and with too high a spirit to be encumbered with your old nonsense."

By nature of being human, we know: 1) we are imperfect, 2) we all suffer, and 3) we all have a shadow self that harbors the rejected, more unpleasant parts of ourselves we wish to hide and deny. Our children often shine the light on our shadow selves when they are angry with us. Or the least attractive parts of ourselves show up when we overreact to the choices they make that we may not agree with or like. We don't want to look at those parts of ourselves, such as our insecurities, short-temperedness, impatience, and rage. That's why we react so strongly—often negatively—when they show up.

It's important that we work to respond both to ourselves and our children with compassion when this happens. I know, that's easier said than done! Compassion is the answer to many things. It is a key ingredient in self-care. Compassion starts with self and then spills over to all of our relationships. We won't parent perfectly. We will mess up. Our kids won't behave perfectly. They too will mess up. Sometimes, when either they or we slip, our response creates shame. Forgive yourself. Have compassion for your humanity. Have compassion for your child's humanity. Our children will experience the same dark feelings and regrets we do. Instead of creating shame by reacting negatively, simply let them know that you see their struggles and are there for them. That doesn't mean you will fix their problems for them or that you approve of their choices. But you can let them know you approve of THEM, even if you don't approve of their BEHAVIOR. Help them trust that "this too shall pass," because whatever it is, it will. *Remember, everything is temporary.* Your children's behavior and their poor choices don't define them, as they don't define you. By feeling compassion for their humanity rather than judging their choices, you and your children can learn to forgive, self-soothe, and problem-solve without the burden of shame. Carrying shame is the heaviest burden of all.

Take a Parenting Break!

We all have bad days as parents. You know those days when we wonder, "What was I thinking when I thought I could parent?" Not only do we have those days, but sometimes those days turn into months or even years. Keep the faith. Try to avoid sinking into shame and stop catastrophizing. We are human. Parenting can be exhausting on a good day, and there are plenty of times when we just don't have it in us. My suggestion for when those moments come is to find time for yourself and take a parenting break. Treat yourself to a mini-vacation, take a walk, meditate, or yes, simply go take a bath! Do not try to hang out with your child during a time when you feel depleted and lost, as this will only end up bringing you both down. My worst parenting moments occur when I don't recognize that I need to take a break and LEAVE for a bit. If I could have some do-overs, there are some situations in which I would definitely choose a parenting vacation rather than staying and reacting negatively out of desperation, frustration, or rage.

I remember a time when one of my kids did something I had asked them not to, and as a result, a piece of nice furniture was damaged. I was furious. I could feel my blood start to boil, and had I stayed in the room with my daughter, I would have lost my mind. So I left the house and started to pace the neighborhood. I was so angry that I couldn't speak. I was determined to stay out long enough to calm down. That took about three hours! I walked into the house only after I had talked myself into understanding that losing my temper would not bring back the furniture. After all, it was only stuff, and what mattered most to me was keeping the integrity of the relationship with my daughter, not the coffee table. I'm not saying that this awareness came to me easily. As I say, it took three hours, but I got there. Unfortunately, most of us just allow our emotions to take over and then have to live with the consequences. Living with the consequences of a damaged relationship is a far heavier burden to bear than living with a damaged coffee table.

I would love to tell you that all of my difficult parenting moments go like this, but they don't. I'm as human as the next mom, and I have been known to yell and scream and carry on too. But I'm not proud of that. And these times rarely, if ever, go well or resolve anything. Typically, I make a bad situation much worse for all involved. This time I had a good day, and one I use to remind myself how I want to parent. There were consequences for my daughter's misbehavior, but they didn't involve shame or belittling her for being a kid and making an irresponsible decision.

Resentment

Most people are confused about what resentment really means. When we feel resentment toward others, it is an indication that we have somehow betrayed OURSELVES along the way. Resentment reminds us that at some point we have not followed our bliss, not honored our gut instincts, not acted in our own best interest, or have allowed others to violate our boundaries. For example, we may feel resentful that we have to drive our kids everywhere, but in reality, that was OUR choice.

Feeling resentment has NOTHING to do with anyone but you. At the moment we start to feel resentment toward someone else, we are veering off course and creating unnecessary anxiety. When we do that, we give the other person all the power. Isn't that silly? Why would we do that? Yet we do it all the time, especially in parenting.

Take a moment and think about what you are feeling resentful about right now. Who is your resentment directed toward? What do you need to do to make a better choice for yourself? Can you decide to let go of the anxiety that holding grudges against others causes and recognize that the real cause of your anxiety is that you did not take a position from a place of self-care?

Once we realize that resentment is not about the other person, we can begin to take steps to correct the choices that led to the feeling in the first place. We can better manage anxiety that was born out of resentment when we realize that resentment is really a betrayal of self. Betrayal of self occurs when we let others dictate what we do, and especially what we feel.

It's important to teach this "resentment is a betrayal of self" concept to our children so they understand that they are responsible for their own feelings and reactions, and that no one has the power to affect them but them. We are all responsible for our own personal journey, choices, and reactions. Our kids will learn this message when we model it for them.

Take a Vacation!

What are some examples of making yourself the priority? How about taking some preventative steps to avoid anxiety build-up—or remedy it? Have you ever gone on a vacation without your kids—just you? Or just you and your partner? Just you and a friend? Consider making this practice a regular part of your vacation planning each year. The next time you have the calendar out, plan a vacation *without* your children. Please. I am begging you. Your children are begging you! They need a vacation from you even MORE than you need one from them. Do yourself and your children a favor and just do it! The parent-child relationship is an intense one. Find a sitter, call a friend, and quit making excuses. Stop the guilt and just GO. We all need a break from one another from time to time. You will come back recharged and refocused, and your kids will appreciate you even more.

Health and Wellness

Another great anxiety buster is to focus on your own health and wellness. Rather than just telling your kids to exercise, why not do it yourself? How about making time for your own yearly check-ups, not just your child's wellness visits? How about eating healthy, organic, whole foods that nourish your body, rather than processed foods that can lead to lethargy or moodiness (at best), and illness or disease (at worst)? Many parent-child struggles are caused by exhaustion and/or nutrition deficits in one or both parties. I have found a great product that helps ensure that my family is getting the nutrition we need. It's called Shakeology (www.shakeassist.com). Shakeology is a delicious, all-natural superfoods shake (I drink the vegan chocolate flavor) that offers a daily dose of dense nutrition. It packs a powerful punch of nourishment, gives us a natural boost of energy, and helps prevent disease. It's been a life saver for us. When the kids don't like the vegan dinner we have prepared, they can always opt for Shakeology!

I also find that hydration plays a key role in behavior. Ideally, we all—kids too—should be drinking water to the tune of about half of our body weight in ounces each day (e.g., if you weigh 180 pounds, drink ninety ounces of water per day!). When my children start to act out or complain that they don't feel well, the first thing I suggest is a tall glass of water. You will be amazed at how many issues this resolves. Remember, the simplest solution is often the best. So the next time you (or your child) feel tired, restless, achy, or dizzy, drink some water first to see if the problem goes away.

Often there is so much going on in a family's life that we end up with poor nutrition, dehydration, and little sleep. Check the calendar and see if you can simplify. How much down time do you and your children get? How many hours of sleep are your kids getting? How many hours are YOU getting? Children and parents need lots of rest and down time. Children may SAY that they want to do a thousand activities, and you may be inclined to encourage that, but don't. Encourage the simple life. Hang out in the backyard and throw a ball around. Sit on the porch and sip lemonade. Sit together on the deck, reading. Kids say they're bored? Looking for something to do? Have them mow the lawn while you take a bath.

Down Time is Not Negotiable

We have become lost in this child-centered world. We need our down time; we need to be alone! Another way of modeling self-care is to put aside a set amount of time each day to be alone in a place where you can listen to your own thoughts and get in touch with your feelings. We need time to think, meditate, calm down, gain perspective, relax, feel, have fun, and simply *be*. We need to do this away from our children and away from our partners, too.

Enjoying alone time seems to be a concept that is lost on the younger generation. In our current climate of "Go, do, produce, succeed," we have lost the pure bliss of being. We seem to have forgotten that we are human beings, not human doings! We need to get comfortable with simply being in a quiet space by ourselves. I hear it all the time: "I have to get home for Junior (who is sixteen!) because he doesn't like to be alone." We are doing our children a great disservice by engaging in this enabling behavior. My theory about why we give in like this is that WE are uncomfortable being alone. I am always amazed that the one suggestion I make in my psychotherapy practice that people resist MOST is quiet meditation. Clients will say, "I'll do ANYTHING except sit quietly with myself!" Let's get one thing clear: silence and quiet is the gateway to peace. Focus on your breathing throughout the day. Take long, full, fill-your-belly-with-air breaths. As we take full breaths, we live a full life. As we take only half a breath, we are living half a life. And obviously, if we take no breath, we have no life. Let's teach our children from a very early age to breathe deeply and be comfortable with—and, dare I say it?—CRAVE quiet. You will be giving them an incredible gift.

There are a myriad of other ways we can show our children how valuable down time can be: take up a hobby, learn to play a musical instrument, clean *your own* room, organize *your own* files, take yourself to the beach or spa or out to dinner and a movie. Or simply go take a bath.

Get a Life!

This entire chapter can be summed up in three words: Get. A. Life. Stop making your kids your primary focus. Doing that is one of the most dangerous errors parents make. Do your children a favor and focus your energy on creating a life of joy, bliss, love, peace, honesty, balance, limits, fun, adventure, healthy eating, exercise, meditation, self-love, self-forgiveness, and self-acceptance. This is a long list, and it could go on and on, but it is achievable. Pour all that goodness over yourself first, and your kids will want the same. Just as flight attendants remind us before takeoff that in case of an emergency, we must first put the oxygen mask on ourselves before assisting our children, we must do the same in our everyday parenting lives, no emergency necessary. In fact, I would say we can avoid some emergencies by adopting this model. Stay conscious of what you are role modeling for your children. Role modeling self-care is the golden ticket in child-rearing.

I know what I'm suggesting is very hard. I struggle with it too, every day. It truly is the road less traveled. In fact, some of my clients have called it radical parenting. But I know that self-care is the key to success. Digging deep for love and compassion, and modeling that behavior for our children, especially when we are at our wits' end, is what matters most.

While what I'm saying is true, so many parents don't or can't practice self-care, even at great cost to the parent-child relationship. Why? Because we can't manage our own anxiety. We must learn how.

Managing Anxiety is Hard, But it's Worth It!

Labor and delivery were hard, but then we had a beautiful baby. College was hard, but then we got a decent job. Painting the kitchen was hard, but now it's beautiful. Working out is hard, but it's necessary to stay strong and healthy, and that feels great. Parenting is no different. It's really hard, mostly because managing our anxiety is REALLY hard. I promise you, the hard work is worth it, and it's definitely the gift that keeps on giving. When the going gets tough, remember the saying, "Be nice to your kids, because someday they'll be picking out your nursing home." It's true. You really do reap what you sow. Do the hard work now and reap all the glorious rewards sooner AND later.

Chapter Three Take-away

Effective parenting requires us to manage our anxiety in order to let our children learn through life experiences. There are many ways to manage parental anxiety. Try some of the ideas presented in this chapter to see what works best for you.

four

Parent Consciously:
Wake Up and Enjoy the Journey

*Mindful parenting is the hardest job on the planet, but it's
also one that has the potential for the deepest kinds of
satisfactions over the life span, and the greatest feelings
of interconnectedness and community and belonging.*
~ *Jon Kabat-Zinn*

Parenting purposefully

We've talked a lot about wholeness, but we haven't delved
into how being whole is connected to the important work of parenting consciously. If you don't stop and think about how you are
choosing to parent, and you remain unwilling to struggle, manage your anxiety, and examine your own vulnerabilities, passing
along your emotional baggage to your children is almost guaran-
teed. Unconscious parenting breeds anxiety, resentment, depression, rage, shame, and feelings of being emotionally smothered
in our children. It simply doesn't work. It creates chaos.

Our goal in parenting is to parent consciously. This means
we make decisions thoughtfully and purposefully, with the best

intentions. We want to avoid reacting emotionally. Here is what conscious parenting looks like:

Child: "Mom, can I go to the party with Julie next Saturday?"
Parent: "Let me think about it. I will get back to you tonight."

Now you may be silently screaming in your head "OF COURSE YOU CAN'T GO TO THE PARTY—HAVE YOU SEEN YOUR ROOM?!" Or let's say your child hits another child on the playground. On the inside you may have an immediate emotional reaction that makes you want to cry, "Billy—YOU COME HERE AND SAY YOU'RE SORRY TO THIS LITTLE BOY!" But instead you respond calmly with, "Let's go to the car and take some time out." This way the child is removed from the situation. You and your child can both calm down in private, and you can decide what to do next. How you choose to handle the situation is not nearly as important as the process of staying calm and responding thoughtfully and purposefully.

Change Your Focus

There is a basic spiritual principle that asserts that what you focus on expands. This is an absolute truth. Often we channel our focus onto a behavior we want to eliminate. That strategy sounds like it makes sense, yet ironically, focusing on this behavior actually exacerbates it. Focus on your child's poor behavior and you get more of the same. Focus on what's wrong on his report card and you get more bad grades. Focus on your child's bad attitude and you only see more attitude. Focus on what's wrong in your life and you just get more problems to add to the list.

So we know what doesn't work; how about we try something else? Instead, focus on all that *is* working and watch that expand!

The more you tell your kids how responsible they are, the more responsible they will become. The more you encourage them to keep up the good work in their friendships, the more great stories they'll have to share. The more you expect them to take care of their own problems, the less they'll expect you to do it for them. *Focus on putting your energy and thoughts into those behaviors you would like to see more of instead of those you want to see stop.* And then observe and enjoy as your whole world shifts and expands into a more beautiful, peaceful place.

Conscious Co-parenting

Whether you are a divorced parent or in a relationship where you and your partner disagree on parenting strategies, trying to parent consciously by yourself can feel incredibly frustrating. You may feel, "What's the point? Everything I do is undone by his father, and I'm always seen as the bad guy."

First, stop this negative thinking. Never underestimate the power you have. How YOU parent matters. And while it may be confusing to a child when he gets different messages from each parent, you can only control what you can control. Trust that you are making an impact. Each parent is responsible for fifty percent of the messages a child receives, and you can only control YOUR fifty percent. Spend your energy making your half the best it can be, and stop taking your partner or ex's inventory. Stop the judgment. The anger, frustration, and disappointment you feel, expressed or not, *WILL be absorbed and felt by your child.* It will not impact the person intended. Choose to focus on the relationship with your child instead of your spouse's behavior.

A friend going through a divorce recently said to me, "My children are far more important to me than a perfect settlement agreement. No amount of money could prevent me from having a good relationship with my ex." It was FAR more important to her to keep the peace and co-parent well than to make sure she got every last dollar she was entitled to. I believe that attitude makes her quite wealthy. By making that simple choice, she will bring loads of good, positive energy into her life that will attract more goodness, light, and abundance. When you consider what she and her children will gain from this way of thinking, it's a no-brainer. What price are *you* willing to pay for peace?

If you are in a situation where you are attempting to co-parent with your ex-spouse or partner, the most important thing your child needs, of course, is for the two of you to work together. If that is truly not possible, the next best option is to speak kindly, or at the very least, neutrally, about your child's other parent. If you name call, criticize, or put down your ex, you are potentially doing irreparable damage to YOUR relationship with your child. Badmouthing your ex-partner backfires nearly all of the time because the child will want to protect the parent being criticized and will turn on the one doing the criticizing. It does not matter whether or not you are speaking the truth. Let your child form her own opinion about the other parent. Do not inject your opinion of the other; stay neutral. Encourage whatever type of healthy relationship is possible and let the rest go. Always work toward speaking to your partner or ex-partner from your highest self to their highest self, regardless of the reaction you get from them. You can only change you, and changing you has the greatest chance of success, period.

Stay Alert to Your Parenting Progress

Are you wondering how your kids experience you? Ask them. It's super fun to get a report card from your children. Periodically I sit down with my kids and ask them for a progress report. What do they love about having me as a mom? What would they change about their childhood if they could? What can I improve upon? I know, this isn't an exercise for the faint of heart, but it is great practice in anxiety management. If you can do it, the benefits are priceless. Their responses will blow you away. Some will make you laugh ("less vegetables, more ice cream"). Some will make you cry ("I wish you didn't get so angry with me"). And some will make you feel proud ("I love how you listen, encourage, and support me"). One thing is for sure: you will get a lot of invaluable information. And when we know better, we do better.

One of, if not THE most important questions you can ask yourself is, "How do my children experience me?" Do they experience me as angry, frustrated, and disappointed? Or do they experience me as joyous, trusting, happy, loving, and warm? Later on, as your children think back to their childhoods, this is what they will most remember. They won't remember each and every parenting decision you ever made. They won't remember the beautifully played parenting choice or even the time you really messed up. They WILL remember the person you were. Did your eyes light up when they walked into a room? Did you have a life that you loved? Were you happy? Did you truly enjoy parenting?

Enjoy parenting. Enjoy your children. Parenting does not have to be stressful every single minute of the day. If we can learn to let go, disengage, support, encourage, and have fun with our kids, parenting can be one of life's greatest pleasures. Often we spend too much time worrying and not enough time savoring the sweetness of the experience. What distracts us from our joy and stresses us out is our need to control it all. STOP. They'll be fine. Enjoy them. If they do something that doesn't work for you, give them consequences. Then go back to enjoying them.

A Word of Warning

The truth is that if you want to parent well, you will often travel a very lonely road. Most parents are parenting unconsciously, but they mean no harm. I have yet to meet a parent who is purposely trying NOT to parent well. They just haven't made the choice to do the hard work. Some people parent unconsciously because it seems easier, but it isn't. It's actually much harder; it just feels easier in the moment. Many parents are just acting on instinct without putting much thought into the long-term consequences of their decisions, so when we choose to parent in an awake state, we will have few companions. Know that before you embark on this journey. It is critical that you are aware of how difficult it will be. Your child may be the odd one out and feel very different from his friends. That's okay. It's yet another opportunity for everyone to practice managing his or her anxiety. And you know what I recommend for that, right? A bath.

How About a Challenge?

Even if you're skeptical, try a hands-off approach for one week. For an entire week, deliberately and consciously choose not to fix the problems your children present. Take lots of baths, read a good book, or plan lunch dates with friends. Above all else, step way back from your normal level of involvement and watch your children's life from a distance. It's only a week—you can do it!

During your week in the balcony, enjoy the show. Watch your children squirm as they problem-solve on their own. Rejoice with them in their successes, empathize with them about how tough life can be when they have setbacks, but please don't fix anything. How will they ever learn that they have the ability and the skills to problem-solve if you always do it for them? How will they learn to cope with life's stressors? They won't, unless they are given the opportunity to practice. Let them practice. Get out of their way.

Does this Work for You?

In the spirit of self-care, before responding to one of the many requests and demands from your child throughout the day, pause, breathe, and think consciously for a moment. Ask yourself, does this request work for ME right now? That is not a typo! I did not say, is it necessary for YOUR CHILD. Look past his demands and consider whether it makes sense for you to respond to him at this moment. I am blown away by how parents respond to their children's requests as quickly as Pavlov's dog responded to the bell for food. Who's in charge? I have many clients who bring their cell phones into sessions, and when they ring they look at me and say, "I just have to check to see if it's the school calling." No, you don't. This is YOUR time. I can guarantee you that whoever is calling can wait the ten minutes you have left in your session.

We do this in small ways all day. We allow our KIDS to dictate our schedules, our menus, our vacations, our moods, what TV shows we watch, etc. Stay-at-home moms in particular often feel it is their "job" to respond to their child's every need. If a child calls from school saying he forgot his lunchbox, it is not your job to get it to him. It's your child's responsibility to remember his own lunch. STOP THE INSANITY. Restructure the hierarchy. Take charge of your own life and your own home. Start by telling your child to wait with his request if it isn't a good time for you. Let him know you won't be able to make his game this week because you have tickets to a show, but you'll catch the next game, and so on.

Embrace Your Vulnerability

Teach your child how to be vulnerable. Vulnerability is the gateway to love, connection, joy, and self-confidence. You teach this by loving yourself, embracing your own vulnerability, and leading by example. How? Let your child see you cry when you feel sad or hurt. Let her see you try even when failure seems the likely outcome. Vulnerability opens the door to building intimate, trusting relationships. Allow yourself to be truly seen by others, for being truly seen will allow you the experience of being loved for the person you are. Role modeling vulnerability is a gift and a legacy you can leave your children that is far more valuable than any amount of money or family heirloom.

Get Clear

Have you ever noticed that your kids give you the hardest time when you are unsure about a parenting decision? Before you make a decision that you know will be unpopular, you need to be clear about it and have confidence that you will be able to follow through. If there's a chance you may waver, you leave yourself open to an abundance of manipulation and whining. When you are crystal clear about your decision, your children can feel your strength and clarity, and therefore are far less likely to challenge you. When *we* get clear, *they* get clear.

Here is a funny and true story to illustrate this concept. When my daughter Arli was an infant, like most babies she did not sleep through the night. Once she had started on cereal and I knew her belly was full, I grew tired of waking throughout the night to comfort her back to sleep. I struggled with the guilt, but the sleep deprivation won out. One evening when I put her down for the night, I kissed her and with utter clarity and confidence in my voice I said, "Arli, if you want to wake up in the middle of the night and cry, 'that's okay,' but I will not be coming in. You are old enough to sleep through the night. I love you and I will see you in the morning." I meant it and she knew it. She never woke up in the middle of the night again! I am not foolish enough to think she understood a word I was saying. What I do believe is that she could feel the clear energy with which I spoke. She got the message loud and clear and didn't argue by testing me.

There is No Such Thing As a Bad Kid

I don't believe in "bad kids." In my years as a parenting coach, I have come to understand that all children want to succeed. They all want to flourish and be happy. Sometimes the environment does not allow that to happen. We are not bad parents. We want the best for our children. But sometimes we simply don't know what that is or how to do it, so our children suffer despite our best intentions.

Sending children to therapy to be "fixed" is usually not the answer. In fact, I believe it often exacerbates the situation by identifying the child as the problem in the family. If you are really interested in helping your children, get parenting skills counseling yourself. You may not be doing anything "wrong." But what you are doing may not work for this particular child. I know that what works for my older daughter certainly does not work for my younger one. If you feel your child needs counseling, I suggest you enroll in parenting coaching sessions at the same time. It's important to discover your piece in the situation and to send the message to your child that this is a family problem, not just an issue with him. Better yet, find a great therapist and start individual psychotherapy sessions. That way you can get to the core of your personal issues that your child continuously triggers.

Chapter Four Take-away

Parents must make conscious decisions in relating to their children and communicate them confidently and clearly. Otherwise we risk knee-jerk, unconscious reactions that can foster anxiety, resentment, depression, shame, and even rage in our children.

five

The Art of Letting Go

Something amazing happens when we surrender and just love.
We melt into another world, a realm of power already within us.
The world changes when we change. The world softens when we
soften. The world loves us when we choose to love the world.
~ Marianne Williamson

What does "letting go" mean anyway? Aren't we supposed to be holding our kids close? Aren't we supposed to protect our children from the scary parts of this world? The answer is yes and no. Yes, love your kids with all of your heart. Let them know how much you care about them. Be there to listen during tough times and hold them close when they're hurting. But no, don't hold on when they want to run free. Don't hold on when they express a desire to be on their own. Don't hold them back from exploring the world because you feel anxious and afraid.

I've noticed that letting go is tougher for some of us than it is for others. However, in my practice, I have observed that the parents who adopt a self-care parenting approach fare far better at letting go than the parents who adopt the kids-first style. The self-care parents worry less because they have their own activities to balance out their lives and keep them from obsessing about their children.

Letting go of your children and the outcomes of their life choices looks different at every stage of their development. When they are babies, we must accept that they may not want to be held right now. In toddlerhood, we must accept that our child may want to put his coat on in a way we don't like. In childhood, we must accept that our children may want to wear inappropriate clothes for the weather or occasion. In adolescence, we must accept that their friends (and just about anyone else) matters more to them than we do. And this pattern continues as our children become adults.

As a psychotherapist, I see many parents who can't let go, and watching this dynamic with their children up close saddens me. Often, parents with adult children struggle the most. These parents can't seem to disengage from their children's lives and don't appear to recognize that their lives and their children's are separate. What strikes me about this is that these parents often remain steadfast in their behavior regardless of the consequences to the relationship. It's as if they have blinders on and can't see the destruction their behavior causes. These parents have never learned to let go. They are searching for attachment and security from their children—perhaps some assurance that they will never be alone. They are looking for their children to meet their needs. It can't be done. Furthermore, it does incredible damage to the children and the parent/child relationship.

This dynamic causes enormous stress and confusion in the relationship as the adult child feels intense loyalty and love for the parent, yet wants desperately to separate so she can create a life of her own. To complicate the matter, these adult children crave independence, but are frequently riddled with fear and anxiety, as they have been trained their whole lives to be dependent on their parent(s). If we don't refocus and work to heal ourselves so that we can allow a natural and appropriate separation to occur, we set our children up for great struggle. This separation needs to start earlier than most people think. I urge you to work on whatever personal fears you have that block you from letting go. Your relationship with your children over the entire course of their lives depends on it.

Let Them Be

Often we want to avoid negative outcomes for our kids. We don't WANT them to fail math. We don't WANT them to be embarrassed or cold when they choose an inappropriate out-fit for the weather or occasion. We don't WANT them to go to bed hungry. We don't WANT them to be arrested. However, the fact is that negative outcomes are amazing growth opportunities because they provide a chance to make a different choice the next time. And negative outcomes at the earliest possible ages are preferred. Better to learn early when problems and consequences are small.

Every time we rob our kids of an unpleasant outcome, we interfere with an organic, soulful process that moves them toward greater maturity. We do this because OUR anxiety, not theirs, gets in the way. Put your energy (and therapy dollars) into learning how to manage your *own* anxiety, not your children's, so you can be more successful at staying out of their way. If you want to participate in a way that's helpful, let your children talk to you. Let them tell you how they are feeling about what they are going through (nod appropriately and show compassion). Communicate to them that you trust that they will get through it and be better for it. Share your own stories of struggle and triumph in order to make a meaningful connection with them.

My wish for you as parents is to let your children go, do, and be. Rather than focusing on the anxiety of everything that can go wrong in a situation where they are asking for more independence, why not rejoice in their newfound freedom? If THEY feel safe enough to try something new, why not trust them? Give them more freedom than you did last year. TRUST THE PROCESS. Manage YOUR anxiety. If your child isn't ready for something, she will tell you. If she says she can handle something on her own, unless she has given you serious reason not to, why not believe her? Trust your kids to figure things out. They will thrive, and their confidence will SOAR when you can let them try some new adventures on their own. As struggles emerge, step back and let them problem-solve so they can take full responsibility for their success. While they are busy taking care of their own lives, get busy taking care of yours.

Back Off!

It is disrespectful to do things for your children that they are perfectly capable of doing for themselves. Examples include, but are not limited to, tying their shoes when they know how, helping with a school project, or calling a teacher to find out about the assignment they missed while out sick. By doing for your children what they can do for themselves, you send the message that you don't believe they are capable of handling things on their own. This is how self-esteem begins to plummet. It's through a series of small, subtle, benevolent, well-meaning gestures that send the wrong message and backfire. Parents do this unknowingly because we love our kids and it's hard to stand by and watch them struggle. Parents intend to send the message, "I love you and I'm here to support you." But that is rarely the message the child receives. Instead the message they take in is, "I don't think you can manage this." Since this affirmation of inadequacy is sent unintentionally, parents are often surprised and bewildered when their children become discouraged. Let your children work out their own challenges so they have the best chance to become strong, confident, competent adults.

Here's an example. Many parents spend a great deal of time focusing on grades, homework, and other markers of academic success with their children. A child comes home with a bad grade on a test or a missed homework assignment, and parents are quick to react—and not in a good way. In my experience, both personal and professional, the greater the parents' investment in a child's academic success, the greater the struggle for the child. I know it sounds counterintuitive, but here's why. Most people think that in order to be responsible parents, they must stay on top of their child's school work. While this assumption may make sense theoretically, if you take a big picture perspective, you will realize that it runs counter to what we have been talking about throughout this book. Once again, parents take too much responsibility, and that results in children taking too little. This scene plays out in homes all over America every day after school. Parents are engaging in one power struggle after the next, and everyone becomes frustrated and angry, all in the name of academic success. Kids will rebel and resist anything that a parent feels emotionally invested in, especially when they enter their developmentally-appropriate rebellious stages.

Instead, imagine if we didn't take much interest in school at all. Sure, go to back-to-school night to meet the teachers and buy your children their necessary school supplies, but then step way back. Let them do their homework or not, pass a test or not, pass sixth grade or not, get a detention or not, study or not. This is not your school experience; it's theirs. By now, I am sure you are aghast at what you've just read and are thinking, "What is this nutty therapist suggesting??? Is she proposing that I not care if my kids are failing school?? Well, she can forget it!" Settle down. That's not what I am suggesting at all. I am offering you an approach that I think will be far more effective at getting your children's grades up than a plan where you are fully engaged, involved, and reactive.

I find that the best approach to parenting is to take an "it's your life" stance. When your children come home with a bad grade on a test, ask how they feel about it. When they forget to do their homework, ask what they feel an appropriate consequence could be for making an irresponsible CHOICE. Notice, I didn't say they were irresponsible. I said they made an irresponsible choice. By making your comments simpler and lighter, and not shaming them by implying that they are irresponsible, you create the greatest chance for change. It's a lot easier for a kid to bounce back from making an irresponsible choice than from being an irresponsible person.

If grades continue to plummet and you feel the need to take a more active role, simply follow through with more significant consequences. The consequences must be delivered without you having a big emotional reaction. Your child may have a fit, and "that's okay." Consequences teach. If you are able to think of a consequence that will really get your child's attention and manage your anxiety so you don't lecture, belittle, or express your dissatisfaction, then I know you will have a great shot at effecting change. The other way (emotional reactivity, frustration, punishment, anger) will not work, especially long-term. I guarantee it. If he does change his behavior for no reason other than to avoid punishment, you've taught him nothing. We want our children to develop a sense of internal motivation that lasts a lifetime. That's only possible if we can step out of their way, and that requires a lot of anxiety management on our part. You can do this!

Don't Let Perfect Get in the Way of Good Enough

If you have a kid who behaves eighty percent of the time, cleans up eighty percent of the time, and is kind to others eighty percent of the time, then I suggest you manage your anxiety the other twenty percent of the time and say nothing. And come to think of it, we don't parent well one hundred percent of the time, so let's cut ourselves the same slack too. Perfection is never the goal. Having a "good enough" parenting experience is what we are after. And we want to teach our children the art of "good enough" living as well.

Since we are not perfect parents, just as our children are not perfect kids, there will come a time or two or a hundred when we feel like we owe our children an apology. Perhaps we embarrassed them unknowingly in front of their friends, or maybe we overreacted to a situation. Maybe we said no too quickly when it was really okay. When those moments occur, we have a glorious opportunity to show our kids our humanity. If we can go to them with honesty and genuinely apologize for our behavior, we will be showing them that it is okay to make mistakes and that we must take responsibility for our choices. What a beautiful gift to give a child. Rejoice when this happens. Be grateful for yet another teachable moment. Your child will cherish it and so will you.

Surrender to the Truth As It Is (Not How You Wish it Were)

The concept of surrender is tough for many to grasp, especially as it relates to parenting. Eckhart Tolle says, "Always say yes to the present moment. What could be more futile, more insane, than to create inner resistance to what already is? What could be more insane than to oppose life itself, which is now and always now? Surrender to what is. Say yes to life—and see how life suddenly starts working for you rather than against you." Please note that in this quote, Tolle does not suggest you accept the present moment only if it is pleasing to you. He proposes accepting it as is because you have no other choice.

If I dare mention the concept of surrender to parents who are in crisis with their children, they become defensive. They react this way because they believe that by suggesting surrender, I am proposing that they give up on their kids. In fact, I am suggesting just the opposite. Never give up on your kids. What I *am* recommending is that we give up on the *crazy* idea that we can control our kids, their choices, and the outcomes of their choices. As parents, we tend to twist and turn and manipulate a situation to make it prettier for us, more palatable, more CONTROLLABLE. The more we argue against reality, the more we suffer. I am advising that we surrender to THE TRUTH, whatever that may be in the moment, and which is likely to change in the next moment. If we surrender to the truth, we have a chance at peace, and so do our kids.

I can't emphasize enough the importance of accepting, speaking, and acting from the truth. Truth-telling is key to success in your parenting journey. Always work toward accepting and speaking the truth in every aspect of your life. Once we understand and accept the truth, knowing what to do next is clearer. Often, once we accept the truth, we learn that our best bet is to surrender to the process. Surrender requires that we trust the process and our children. When we don't trust the process or surrender to the truth, we set ourselves and our children up for emotional difficulties.

What does surrender look like? Let's say Sally comes home from school with a note that says she must stay late because she didn't turn in her homework, and when confronted, she spoke freshly to the teacher. Surrender. Say, "Okay." Don't dive in and try to fix the situation. Don't call the school. Don't pile on the consequences. Surrender. "But what if the school is wrong?" you ask. "What if my child didn't talk freshly and there was a misunderstanding between the teacher and my child?" Surrender. It's okay. Let it go. Let your child work it out. And if she can't work it out, surrender to the idea that she may have to serve an undeserved detention. Surrender to the idea that she will survive this, because she will. And she will be better for it, because life isn't always fair. The "life isn't always fair" lesson is another one to teach early and often.

Trust the Process

Often parents ask me for assurances that they are making every right parenting decision, especially when things get complicated and stressed. So many muddied parenting dilemmas come up over the course of raising a child. I am here to tell you that there are no "right" answers, and I don't claim to know what is or isn't right for your child. What I do know is that there is a greater process at work. I call it God. You may not. But I know that when we parent from a conscious place and make self-aware, thoughtful, non-reactive choices along the parenting journey, things typically end well. It's not always sunshine and light along the way, and this self-care approach is no guarantee that things will go swimmingly all of the time. But I can assure you that as we muddle through this parenting mire, we need to trust our kids, trust ourselves, and most important, trust the process. Trusting the process is key to moving through this complicated parenting journey with as little drama as possible.

Detaching with Love

Just because we relinquish the idea that we can control our children, their choices, and the consequences of their choices doesn't mean we stop cheering for them or fiercely loving them. What it does mean is that "love" truly becomes a verb. Detaching with love is literally love in action. It's easy to love our kids when things are going well. But it's not always effortless to behave in a loving way when it feels like everything is falling apart. In fact, sometimes it's nearly impossible to do so when we are at our wits' end. This is precisely when we must detach with love. Detaching is loving to your child because it puts the full responsibility for his life squarely on his own shoulders. Your child becomes responsible for the successful outcomes resulting from a tough time in his life, and he also gets to take full responsibility for negative outcomes. Emotionally detaching is loving to ourselves because it releases us from the notion that we can influence our child's life situation. Believing that we have control when we really don't is an unnecessary and heavy burden to bear.

When our child experiences a negative outcome, either by his actions or inactions, watching him struggle can feel excruciating. It is especially agonizing when we have many thoughts about how he could have avoided the whole darn thing in the first place. It is critical to detach, let go, and let it be. Al-Anon, a support group for family and friends of problem drinkers, often discusses the concept of detaching with love. It is important for loved ones to understand that the burden of responsibility falls on the drinker, not on family or friends. Members support each other in accepting the idea that we can continue to love someone, yet create emotional distance in the relationship. We can love them, and we can detach from taking responsibility for their choices and trying to fix them. Sometimes, in extreme cases, detachment can mean a temporary pause in a relationship. The situation may be such that we need to take a break from the person's life for a while. This is often necessary when the choices our children are making are simply too difficult for us to watch and endure up close.

But more often it's not necessary to go to this extreme. Usually we don't need to cut off from our children in order to emotionally detach from them. We can say to ourselves, "This is not my problem. I feel sad watching my child struggle, but there is nothing I can do to prevent it. I can express my love and good wishes for her and then back out of telling her what to do. I trust that she can figure this out. I also trust that if she can't figure it out, she can cope with whatever consequences follow." The key, again, is to trust the process.

Patience

We can't talk about letting go, surrendering, and detaching with love without talking about my own Achilles' heel: patience. This one is super tough for me. I have struggled with patience all my life. I have always wanted whatever I wanted RIGHT NOW, as my dad and husband will tell you. I can't stand to wait, and I can't stand to be told that I must wait (no idea where my daughter Zoe gets it from). You can bet that this personal vulnerability shows up in my parenting all the time. It is hard enough to surrender, or watch your child struggle, or detach with love, when you have an easy-breezy personality. Imagine how hard it is for someone like me who was born without the patience gene.

I watch those of you who have loads of patience with awe. My friend Amy demonstrates many examples of patient parenting. I have witnessed this woman patiently and quietly watch her child have a temper tantrum and stay as calm as I look when I am in deep meditation on a beach in Mexico. Frankly, I don't know how you patient people do it. My whole life has presented me with one exercise in patience after another. God knew EXACTLY what he was doing when he sent Zoe in my direction. But as I've said, Zoe is here to teach me patience. I know that, and on most days, I am grateful. It is said that when you pray for patience, God sends you the opportunity to practice it. Thanks for the daily lessons, God. I REALLY appreciate them.

So I do not speak to you about this topic from a place of mastery. I speak to you from the trenches. However, I can tell you that patience is required in order to parent from a place of self-care. Nothing moves quickly in parenting (except the years, I suppose). But the day-to-day struggles of parenting take a lot of dedication and patience. The lessons of love we are teaching our children require them. When I can feel my patience supply running low, I can almost visualize a red flag that tells me I am not doing enough to refuel myself spiritually or emotionally. I am not paying enough attention to my own needs. I am not practicing enough self-care. Maybe I need a night out with my husband. Maybe I need a night out with my girlfriends. Maybe I need to take a long walk, exercise, or meditate. But I know that when I am losing patience, it's about me, not my child. She's just doing the job she was sent here to do. Oh, and she does it WELL! She is a living doll who offers me daily practice at managing my greatest vulnerability. Once I master it, she won't need to work so hard.

Think about how patient you are. Is this your strength or your vulnerability? If it's your strength, good for you! You are armed for this journey in a way many of us are not. If, like me, it's your vulnerability, run, don't walk to the nearest therapist, meditation studio, or yoga class.

You Are Not the Social Director of Your Child's Life

It is not your responsibility to entertain your children. An important life skill that they need to master by the time they are adults is to take personal responsibility for themselves, and this includes taking responsibility for their own good time. If they are above the age of eight, have them plan their own play dates and ask you for permission or a ride. Do not feel obligated to find things to entertain them. This includes video games and other technology. Simply say, "It's beautiful outside. No technology today." When they balk, ignore them. When they whine, ignore them. When they yell, "But there's NOTHING TO DO OUTSIDE!" ignore them. Resist the urge to fix things for them. Again, your own anxiety management is critical. If you seriously can't take their boredom and the whining that accompanies it, go take a bath. And may I suggest you bring in some music to drown out the noise.

Focus on Quality Time

Working parents need not worry that their children are getting less of them or in some way getting the short end of the stick. It is the quality of time, not the quantity of time that matters most. There are awesome stay-at-home moms and dads and wonderful working parents too! Do not judge yourself or feel guilty because you chose one path over the other. Focus instead on the quality of the interactions between you and your child. Stay calm. Enjoy parenting. Remember, what's most important is that you choose a path that brings you happiness. Your life satisfaction is what your child most needs. Don't waste a second feeling guilty because you work outside the home. Guilt is one of those wasted emotions and energy drainers that leads to poor parenting choices. Don't get sucked in.

Here's a challenge: Take fifteen minutes each day to give your child uninterrupted, focused attention. Play a board game, throw a ball around, take a walk, or simply have a conversation. Make a big deal about it, for example by turning off cell phones and computers. Make sure to tell your children how much you are looking forward to spending time with them.

But They're Only Young Once!

In my psychotherapy practice, I am often struck by how resistant parents are to encouraging their children to become more and more responsible for themselves. I wonder what parents could possibly object to. What I have come to understand is that many parents feel that life is hard enough. Since they love their children so much, they want to do whatever they can to ease the burdens of their formative years. I hear, "They're only young once. They have a lifetime to master these skills." I disagree. They actually have a small window of time to master these coping skills. Sure, I suppose your children can figure it out the hard way as adults, but why would you subject your adult children to such hardship and say you're doing it in the name of love? How is making their lives harder loving? Why not teach them from the moment they come into this life that you TRUST them to figure things out on their own? We are here to be their coaches, cheerleaders, and supporters. I like to think of parenting as bumper bowling. As parents, we will prevent you from heading for the gutter, but other than that, it's on you. We are not here to manage your anxiety; we are here to manage our own.

Encourage Independence

From the moment our children are born, we need to prepare them for independence. That's our primary job and responsibility. So ask yourself, "What skills will my child most need to live a fulfilling, successful life?" Once you have the answer to this question, parenting decisions come much more easily. Often we get so caught up in our OWN anxiety that we lose sight of our basic goal in parenting: prepare to launch!

How do you put kind, independent, loving humans who absolutely love life out into the world? You provide enough love and structure to help them feel safe, enough independence to help them feel confident, enough joy to keep them smiling, enough challenge to keep them thinking, and enough down time to keep them sane. Developing well equipped adults requires struggle in childhood. Children develop coping skills by working through life's challenges. Let them labor a bit and have faith that they will succeed triumphantly. Maybe they won't succeed the first time, but trust that eventually they will.

When I ask adults in my psychotherapy practice about how they feel or what they want, they often don't know. This is probably because they were never asked these questions as children. Today many children are being micromanaged—growing up being told what to wear, how to feel, how to behave, when they should feel hungry, etc. Do your children a huge favor and teach them to develop their own sense of self. This is done simply by asking questions instead of telling them what to do, think, and feel.

> Your child: "Mom, what should I wear today?"
> You: "What would you like to wear?"
> Your child: "Dad, I don't know how to ask my math teacher about taking a makeup test."
> You: "What do you think you could say?"

Give them a chance to learn who they are and what they need. By asking questions instead of telling them how YOU would do it, you give them an opportunity to develop a sense of who THEY are, how THEY feel, and what THEY want in life. They also learn to develop problem-solving skills that they'll have for a lifetime!

We want our children to become responsible, mature, self-confident adults. Therefore, we must let them make their own choices and take age-appropriate, responsible actions. We are constantly doing things for our kids that they are perfectly capable of doing themselves. Let them tell the waitress what they want to order at the restaurant. Let them call the library to see if the book they want is available. My daughter did this at age eight (with me at her side). Let them call the orthodontist to schedule an appointment when they break a bracket. There is no better way to create adults who can make decisions than to let them practice under our supervision. Let's replace "I'll take care of it!" with an enthusiastic and encouraging, "You can do this!"

I am a big believer in launching your children into independence as early as possible. For example, when your preteen begins to express a desire to stay home alone, I say allow it. Obviously, this will depend greatly on your child's maturity level, but if she is expressing a desire to stay alone for short bursts of time, I encourage you to give her a chance. Again, this is another exercise in managing your own anxiety and trusting the process. But I think this particular leap of faith is well worth it. It really helps your child develop into a more responsible person, and the good feelings she will get from it are priceless. If she doesn't feel ready, "that's okay." But as she starts to get older, begin to insist, even if only for a few minutes to start. It's critical that she learn this important life skill.

Another way to cultivate independence is to involve your kids in all of the household chores. If they're old enough to walk and they're old enough to talk, then they're old enough to help. Let your five-year-old push the vacuum cleaner around. Let your ten-year-old help you prepare dinner. Even your two-year-old can learn how to pick up her toys and put them away. Not only does participating in chores teach your children valuable life skills, it also builds their self-confidence. It gives them an I-can-do-it attitude and takes the parental burden of juggling all of the chores and spreads it around. In my opinion, it's best to start early. If it's always expected that they help, it won't be so difficult to get them to empty the dishwasher or mow the lawn as they get older.

Often you hear people say that we need to raise the bar for our kids. I agree, but I mean it differently from most people. I think we need to raise the bar, but not in terms of their extracurricular activities, or even their scholastic achievements. I believe we need to raise the bar in terms of personal responsibility. We need to increase our expectations that they can handle their own life struggles and problem-solve for themselves. We need to raise the bar on what we expect them to contribute to the family, the community, and the world.

Launching Over the Lifespan

We must always have this thought at the forefront of our minds throughout the parenting journey: How will this help my child manage in adulthood? Start this thinking from the moment your child is born.

When they are infants, we teach them that they are okay in their crib away from Mom and Dad for a few hours. In toddlerhood, we step a few feet away from our child who is petting a friendly dog. And this "you're okay" message continues when

Go Take a Bath! | 71

we send them to school, a play date, overnight camp, a prom, driver's education, college, marriage, etc.

We feel most challenged in those years when our kids are between four and forty, when we most want them to internalize the notion that they are capable of handling life's struggles on their own. Ask yourself, is this something they can do without me? Note that I didn't ask if they WANT to do it without you; I asked if they are capable. I didn't ask if you *mind* doing it; I asked if *they* are capable. If they are capable of handling something on their own, even if they will do it with some struggle, I recommend you back off. Encourage skills that prepare them to launch. If this causes you too much anxiety, seek professional assistance. I don't say that to be flippant. I say that because it is CRITICAL to your children's development that you manage your anxiety enough to allow them to struggle through uncharted territory under your tutelage.

It's Never Too Early and It's Never Too Late to Start Letting Go

Your home should be a living laboratory, a microcosm of the real world. And in the real world, some very specific life skills are required. I think of my home and my parenting as a classroom set up to teach my children to live full, responsible, independent lives. If the living room needs to be vacuumed or the dishwasher needs to be emptied, we share the chores. If my kids want to buy something they want but don't need, they must earn the money to make that happen. If they want to place a book on hold at the library, I teach them how to find the phone number and encourage them to give the library a call. If they need to be coached about what to say because they've never done it before, I coach them. If they are struggling with friendships, I teach them relationship skills. If they are having trouble with a teacher and they disagree with a grade, I encourage them to go speak to the teacher. Why would I speak to the teacher? Whose life is it anyway?

By encouraging your children to do things for themselves, you allow them to build confidence. *Confidence is developed and strengthened by doing difficult things that are out of their comfort zones and being successful.* Maybe they won't be successful the first time, but eventually they will. Then they will realize, "Oh, I CAN do this on my own!" and that feels AMAZING to a child. It feels amazing to all of us! Feeling capable is a critically important life skill. When we don't feel capable, we make decisions out of fear, feelings of inadequacy, dependency, and low self-worth. The formula to help your kids feel capable is simple: let them do it on their own! Prepare to launch! Regardless of your child's age, start now. Even if you have an adult child struggling with independence issues, start now. It is never too late. It's just much easier the earlier you begin.

When my older daughter started kindergarten, I had a lot of anxiety to manage. I was anxious about letting her launch into this new world of public school. I knew what the world was like, and I knew it looked a lot different from our home environment. I wasn't ready for her to know it too. So, because God has such a wonderful sense of humor and couldn't wait to challenge me, Arli arrived home from her very first day of kindergarten with a story. "Mom, Katie kicked my book bag," she said. "WHAT!?" was how I was feeling. I wanted to march right in there and tell that Katie a thing or two. How DARE she do that to MY daughter! This girl obviously doesn't know who she's dealing with! I wanted to call Katie's mother! I wanted to call the teacher! I wanted to speak to the principal! That is how strongly I was reacting inter-nally. I am no different from any other mother. I can't stand to see my child struggle—especially when the situation is so unfair and unkind, like this one. But because I am committed to a conscious, self-care approach to parenting, and because I am trying to launch my child into independence, I did not act out of that anxiety. Instead, I took a breath, then another one. I continued to do deep breathing until I could say, "How would you like to handle that?" There. I said it. I just spit it out even though every cell of my being was freaking out. I was proud. Her response? "If she does it again, I am going to tell her to stop, and if she still doesn't, I am going to talk to the teacher." And there you have it.

One More Thing About Letting Go

To illustrate how our own childhood vulnerabilities affect our parenting reactions and choices, I offer the following personal example.

I was a latchkey child growing up. So by third grade, I was walking home and letting myself in with my key, which was hanging around my neck with a shoelace. I would go into the house and watch television until my dad would arrive home from work. This was very normal to me, so I don't consciously remember feeling particularly scared or anxious about it.

Just because I don't remember doesn't mean I didn't feel that way, though. When I became a mother for the first time, I suddenly felt very protective and wanted to make sure that my daughter, Arli, never felt alone or abandoned. I was hyper-conscious in making sure she felt profoundly cared for and loved, and I was especially diligent about making sure that she felt my presence as a parent. Remember, my mom left our home when I was only eight years old, so I was hypersensitive to the idea of being a maternal presence for my only daughter at the time. This need to be present and make sure Arli never felt alone or abandoned was an easy anxiety to manage, mostly because I was always home when she got off the bus, or I arranged appropriate child care if I was working or otherwise unavailable.

One day when Arli was in kindergarten, I was out running errands. I was aware of the hour, so I left myself plenty of time to beat the bus. However, ten minutes before the bus was due to arrive at my house, I found myself sitting in traffic that had the potential to make me late. The bus had already left school, so I couldn't contact anyone to ask that she be held there. So I was left to manage my own anxiety. She was five years old, remember, not fifteen. And as I said, I was already struggling with anxiety about sending her into the world anyway. This situation was not helping.

I grabbed my cell phone and frantically began calling all of my neighbors, but naturally, no one was home. My heart started beating really fast and I started to sweat. All I could think about was how my precious, innocent five-year-old would manage until I got home. What will she be feeling when the bus arrives and she doesn't see my car? Keep in mind that I was about thirty seconds to two minutes behind the bus at this point. These feelings were totally irrational based on what was actually happening. However, in my mind, I was the five-year-old, scared and alone.

I finally got past the traffic and started gunning the gas to get home as quickly as I could. As I started to travel down my street, I could see the bus just ahead of me. I raced faster to get ahead of it, but despite herculean efforts, I couldn't do it. My most dreaded fear was about to come true. My five-year-old daughter was going to get off the school bus and face an empty house. She was going to arrive home with no one to greet her, no one to hug her, and no neighbors to be found. Although, in my attempt to talk myself out of anxiety, I realized we were now talking about only thirty seconds of what I was convinced would be sheer terror for my little girl. But that thought offered little comfort.

I raced around the corner and screeched into my driveway, heart pounding and sweat pouring off my brow. I started honking frantically yelling, "HI!!!!!!!!!!!! HI, ARLI!!!!!" It's MOM, sweetie! I'm here now! I'm so sorry!" All I can tell you is that she looked at me like I had just pulled up in a sailboat. Her five-year-old face was saying, "What a drama queen. Why is this nutty woman screaming?" I ran over to her, crying (me, not her), and hugged her tightly. Once I had unlocked my death grip, I asked her how she was feeling. Her response was to look at me strangely and say "Fine." I said, "What would you have done if I hadn't pulled up just then? What would you have felt? Were you scared?" She calmly explained (taking a maternal role) that she would have walked over to the neighbors' houses until she found someone home, and that she knew I would be home any second so she wasn't worried.

As parents, when we are not consciously separating our issues from our children's, these scenes are common. Our issues are not their issues. It is dangerous to project our anticipated reactions, based on our own past ones, onto them. This was a pretty benign story, and the consequence was nothing more than my child thinking I was crazy for a moment, a rapid heartbeat, and sweat on my brow. But it is a clear example of what it looks like when we behave out of our own childhood pain instead of what is actually happening. Our reaction, as mine was, is usually over the top and unnecessary and can cause our children increased anxiety that was never theirs in the first place. We project our anxiety onto them. And because they are so young and impressionable, they take it on as truth. How sad!

I am happy to report that this was an isolated incident. I got a grip on myself fast. But what if I hadn't quickly become aware of my behavior? What if this was just one of hundreds of similar over-the-top reactions? Can you see how I would be training my daughter to feel afraid? Can you imagine how if that scene were a familiar one, I could be getting in the way of her developing into an independent woman? Take a moment right now to think about your own vulnerabilities from childhood. Ask yourself how you manifest those vulnerabilities with your own children. Remember, you don't have to be a perfect parent to raise independent, self-sufficient, self-confident adults; but you do need to be a conscious one. Becoming aware of your vulnerabilities and taking direct action to separate your own anxieties from your children's will go a long way toward getting you to your parenting goals.

Chapter Five Take-away

Our children can't become whole without struggle. No matter how painful it feels to us, we must let go and let them learn for themselves. If we feel incapable of letting go because we feel too afraid, we must seek out a professional to help us work through our fears.

six

Create Win-Win Situations: Boundaries, Limits, Rules, Roles, and Choices

The rules for parents are but three...love, limit, and let them be.
~ Elaine M. Ward

In every family system, as with any solid organization, there must be an executive committee, and parents are it. When it comes to raising self-sufficient, resilient, confident kids, we need to find the balance between giving them the power they seek *without* giving away our own power as parents and our position on the executive committee. We do that by setting limits, creating boundaries, and enforcing rules.

Power Struggles

Children misbehave to get power or attention, and frankly, most of the time, it's power they're after. They wake up every morning with one purpose: to win every power struggle. And they have all day to do it. You, on the other hand, have things to do, places to go, and people to see. Therefore, you WILL tire first. Face it: you're in quite a pickle. Since you can't win anyway, challenge yourself to *unhook* from every power struggle/argument in which they attempt to engage you.

You don't have to argue these mini-battles; you own the place. You have already won. Use your REAL power, not your size and volume, to get your point across. You can disengage from every power struggle by starting your first sentence with "That's okay." Some examples: "That's okay. You don't have to do your homework, but you can't go out until you do." "That's okay. You don't have to wash your clothes, but I won't be doing it." "That's okay. You don't have to clean your room, but I won't be taking you to dance class until you do." "That's okay. You don't have to eat that, but I'm not making anything else." When they have a fit, go take a bath.

When You Say No, Do You Really Mean It?

When children hear the word no and react with lots of begging and pleading, parents often give in. If this scenario sounds familiar, be aware that the message you're sending is "Never take me seriously, and everything is negotiable." What? That wasn't the message you meant to send? Intermittent reinforcement, in this case sometimes giving in after you've made a different decision, is one of the most powerful influencers of human behavior. Giving in sporadically is exactly what causes your child to keep on trying. She thinks, "Last time it took three hours of begging before Mom/Dad gave in. All I need to do is keep at it." So get clear on your answer first. Are YOU certain that the answer is no? If you are, then go ahead and state your answer clearly, one time. At this point, you can offer up a short explanation. After that, ignore all future conversation, and if she persists, continue to ignore her as you draw yourself a bath.

Choose Battles Wisely

Most battles just aren't worth the hassle. However, if you want to put your foot down, make sure you're doing it for something that really matters. To increase your chances of being heard, make this kind of reaction a rare event. If everything is a battle, your child will be unable to tell what's really important to you and what isn't. Think long and hard before you act. By taking a stand *rarely*, you train your child's brain to understand, "Oh boy, this must be important! I'd better listen because usually my parents let me figure this stuff out on my own."

Less is More

Although it may seem counterintuitive, I suggest saying very little to your children when you want to teach them something important. When you say too much, the words become white noise in their brains. They can't hear you. They can't focus. However, if you say one thing, one very important sentence such as, "That doesn't fit with our family's values" or "That's not the choice I would make" and then be quiet, you're onto something. Because when you make one significant point and then walk away, their brains will spin and circle back to that one point over and over again. Your brief words will do all of the heavy lifting for you. This is a far more effective approach in getting your point across, and far better than repeating yourself over and over (and over!).

Natural and Logical Consequences

The best consequences are natural or logical ones. A natural consequence is one that requires no intervention from us. You don't eat, you feel hungry. You ride your bike too fast, you fall. You drink when you're under age, you get arrested. It's great when the universe intervenes on our behalf. When these types of consequences occur, our best approach is simply to step out of the way and let life teach our kids. Parents find not intervening in the natural consequences their children experience very challenging, but there is no better way to learn.

If natural consequences are not an option, then logical consequences are your next best bet. Logical consequences link the misbehavior to a logical result. "If you don't stop watching TV when time is up, you lose TV privileges." "If you come in an hour late today, you must come home an hour early tomorrow." "If you won't take your sister to dance class, you can't use my car." "If you stay up too late tonight, you have to go to bed early tomorrow." However, consequences that are unrelated to the misbehavior teach nothing. Our kids express anger and disappointment, but behavior change is unlikely. Instead of, "You are grounded/punished because you didn't clean the kitchen as you were asked," instead try, "You can go out any time after the kitchen is cleaned." He doesn't want to? "That's okay, but you can't go out until it's done." Who cares? Not you, I hope. Because if you do, you will engage in a power struggle in which you are destined to lose and from which you will feel exhausted. I beg of you, don't bite.

Consequences help your children learn from their choices. Punishment only teaches them to stop the undesired behavior because of the shame it creates. Shame is cancer of the soul.

We can avoid punishing our children by keeping our tone neutral, not overreacting, and imposing natural and logical consequences. We know we have moved away from consequences and into punishment if our voices are raised, our tones are angry, or we express frustration and disappointment. It is critical to your children's emotional development and to your relationship with them that you avoid punishing them. If you find this suggestion nearly impossible, I encourage you to seek professional assistance. Your inability to refrain will have devastating consequences for your child, and will likely result in feelings of guilt and discouragement on your end.

When giving your child a consequence for misbehavior, it's important to remember that the consequence is intended to *teach* rather than *punish*. Discipline comes from the word disciple, which means "to teach." Thus, most consequences should not last longer than twenty-four hours. The goal is to teach your child a way to do better the next time. He can't learn a better way if "next time" isn't for a week or a month because he's been grounded. Plus, by keeping the consequence short-term, it will be fresh in his mind, and the chances are greater that he won't want to repeat the behavior that led to the consequence. Phrase the consequence so it's clear that HE CHOSE it when HE CHOSE to break a rule. You aren't punishing him. He simply made a choice that led him to a very predictable, yet unfortunate, outcome. "I noticed you didn't turn off the TV when I asked, and as a result, you have decided to have no TV for twenty-four hours. You will get a chance again tomorrow to show me that you can listen when I ask you to do something." NO ANGER is the key; simply follow through.

If you feel in your gut that your child needs a consequence for something, go with that feeling. Often parents tell me they had a concern with a choice their child made, but they couldn't do anything about it because they couldn't "prove it." This is not a court of law. You don't need to prove anything. You are a parent. You have instincts. And if your gut is saying that something happened, it probably did. Proceed accordingly.

Discipline, to be truly effective, requires us to be kind and firm. We are on their side. We are rooting for them to make the choice that gives them the most freedom. We want them to live their lives and enjoy themselves. There is no need to set up an "us vs. them" dynamic. If they can't get their homework done, or vacuum the kitchen floor, or empty the dishwasher as they've been asked, "that's okay." But they have also made the choice not to go to the party, or the baseball game, or the prom, or wherever. We can wish from the sidelines that they had made a different choice, but we need to allow them to feel the consequence of the choice they made for themselves. *Discipline is about not arguing or giving in.*

The Power of Choice

Children want control, so give it to them! But do so in appropriate ways. Give your child the power to choose his own path. After all, that's really what we all want. We want the ability to choose our own direction in life. That seems fair, doesn't it? Children, like adults, don't like to feel controlled. And like adults, they tend to rebel if they feel that way.

But you can have your cake and eat it too: offer your children choices within limits. This strategy keeps you in charge and gives them freedom at the same time. So you can say, "Do you want to clean your room now or after lunch?" "Do you want to cook dinner tonight or tomorrow night?" "Do you want to do your homework now or after dinner?" "It's time to nap. Do you want to walk or be carried to your room?" The more you can create a choice *within* a limit, the greater chance you have at dismantling a power struggle at the source. Your child's brain is so busy making a choice, he forgets to argue with you. In this way we can set limits AND give choices. This approach stops the cycle of arguing and gives children the power they crave.

Reward and Punishment vs. Choice and Consequence: What's the Difference?

Most parents use reward and punishment as their primary form of discipline. A reward is typically a material gift given in exchange for cooperation, good behavior, or achievements. Thus, reward teaches children to expect "payment" for their cooperation. Some examples are: "If you're good at the mall, I will buy you ice cream," or "If you get straight A's, I will buy you a car." Punishment, on the other hand, occurs when you overreact, respond with anger or frustration, or when the consequence is not linked to the misbehavior. Punishment is shaming to a child of any age, even an adult child.

Often, parents don't understand the difference between a punishment and a consequence and view this distinction as mere semantics. They often tell me, "You call it consequences; I call it punishment. What's the difference?" These two concepts are totally different and produce very different results. Not understanding this distinction is exactly what causes so much parental stress and frustration. It is one of the most common reasons children act out.

Punishment teaches your child nothing about making a different choice next time. Typically, it teaches him to feel anger, shame and fear. On the other hand, natural and logical consequences DO work very effectively at helping children of all ages make better choices. The strategy of natural and logical consequences communicated with a matter-of-fact, calm, neutral,

I-don't-care-which-one-you-choose attitude is my definition of effective discipline.

To illustrate this point, I ask you to imagine driving 55 mph in a 25-mph speed zone because you are late to work. When you are pulled over by the policeman, he begins to scream at you. "What the HELL do you think you're doing??!! What is WRONG with you? Do you know the speed limit on this street, or are you new around here? Let me see your license!" When you take out your license, you begin to shake because of how belittled you feel. As you timidly show it to him, he continues to berate you. "I see you live right down the street. I'm sorry, but there is NO excuse for this behavior. NO EXCUSE!" And off he goes, angrily walking to his car to write you a ticket. When he returns with your ticket, he throws it at you and storms away. At last you can finally get away from this lunatic and call a friend. What do you imagine you might say to this friend? I'm guessing you would tell your friend about this nutty police officer and how enraged you feel about how you were treated. Am I right? In this scenario, you are so preoccupied with the officer that you have barely thought about your own poor choice and the consequence that followed: the ticket. This is a classic example of punishment.

Now imagine the same scenario, only this time you have the kindest cop in the world. He calmly approaches the car with a warm, friendly smile. He asks how your morning is going. You exchange a few pleasantries. After a few minutes, he gently asks to see your driver's license. You gladly oblige. He too returns from his car with a speeding ticket. However, he hands it to you without any drama and wishes you a better day. He encourages you to drive safely because he doesn't enjoy giving out tickets to such nice people this early in the morning. You both smile at his attempt to soften the blow, and you both drive away. It was clear from his attitude and behavior that he wished he didn't have to give you a ticket, but for your own safety, he had to. He wishes you had made a different choice, but you didn't. "That's okay;" maybe next time. In this scenario, when you call a friend, what do you think you would want to talk about? My guess is that you wouldn't even mention the police officer at all as you would probably be focused on your own poor choice—speeding—and having to pay this ticket. You would be focused on your behavior and the consequence that followed. You'd be thinking about how you would be likely to make a different choice next time. This scenario is a classic example of a consequence.

Do you see the difference between these two scenarios? Do you think it's just semantics? Although the ticket was the same in each, in the first scenario, you were focused on the *person* delivering the consequence (the ticket). If you are focused on the *person* delivering a consequence, you can bet you've been punished (shamed). In the second scenario, you were focused on your own poor choice and resulting commitment to make a better one in the future. This calmer and more constructive response is only possible when we experience consequences instead of punishment.

Learning is only possible when you are not distracted by the other's behavior. In the first scenario, in which the police officer was rude, angry, overreactive, disrespectful, and condescending, you were NOT thinking about what you would do differently next time. In fact, I'll bet you would have told a LOT of people about the angry police officer and very little about the ticket or your own behavior.

This happens in parenting ALL THE TIME! Parents get angry, and kids don't change their behaviors or learn from the consequences because they were never consequences at all. What they got were punishments. Children don't learn from punishments. If your goal is to help your child make better choices in the future, I strongly encourage you to manage your reactions and simply hand out logical consequences or allow natural consequences to occur without your intervention. Trust that your child will respond to these far better than emotionally reacting to his poor choice, grade, or attitude. This approach is your best chance to get his attention, and it has the best odds of achieving your desired outcome.

A "Consequences" Story Featuring Yours Truly

To illustrate the differences between punishment (bad) and consequences (good) and the effects each have on us, I offer the following personal story.

Several years ago (before I discovered Shakeology), I had something seriously wrong with my left foot that resulted in my needing a cast. My doctor was located in center city Philadelphia, where parking is scarce and expensive. As I was driving down the highway to get to the appointment, I encountered an accident that had blocked traffic for miles. It was clear that I was going to be very late for an appointment I had waited months to obtain. I started to panic and called the office to explain the situation. "No problem," they said, "but you need to be here by 3:00 p.m. because we leave then." So I continued to sit in traffic wondering if I should just turn around and head home since it was a gamble whether I would make it on time. Finally, the traffic cleared, and I arrived at the office location at 2:45 p.m. Great, except that I couldn't find a parking space or lot close enough to get me checked in at the office within fifteen minutes. Thinking quickly and feeling flustered, I made my first stupid decision of the day when I decided to park in a handicapped spot. My plan, which made sense to me at the time, was to run upstairs to check in and then run back down to my car to find a more suitable place. I would only be in the spot for less than five minutes. I couldn't imagine that I would get a ticket in that short amount of time. Boy, was I wrong!

After checking in, I went back to my car to find a ticket on my windshield to the tune of $60. I figured that I had just paid very handsomely for parking, so I left the car where it was and went back upstairs to my appointment (stupid decision #2). When I finished my appointment and came downstairs, I found that my car had disappeared. Disappeared! Nothing like this had ever happened to me. At first, I made the assumption that it had been stolen. But after some time, I realized that my car had been towed! I could not believe it. I was alone, angry, confused, and scared. I had NO idea what I was supposed to do next. None. I didn't know who to call or where to go, and it was getting cold and dark.

After walking in circles and crying on and off, I started asking people on the street some questions and they directed me to a cab driver. He took me to the impound lot where they take all the cars whose owners make dumb parking choices. The cab driver got a kick out of my naiveté and made a lot of silly jokes on our way. They weren't enough to lighten my mood, but his kindness helped me keep things in perspective.

When I arrived at the impound lot, I stood in a long line. It was starting to get really dark by then, and my fear level was rising. I finally got to the front of the line and explained to the woman behind the glass what had happened. I expected her to look at me with disdain (seriously, what decent person parks in a handicapped spot and expects to get away with it?). However, I was surprised at how kind and helpful she was. She explained that when I saw that I had a ticket, I should have moved the car immediately. DUH! I get that now, but at the time my plan and rationalization made perfect sense. I was, in fact, disabled—remember? I had a cast on my foot, for heaven's sake! And I already had to pay a $60 ticket! I owned that spot as far as I was concerned. But, lesson learned. It won't happen again; let me just pay my $60 fine and go. I figured I would have a funny story to tell the kids and husband when I got home. I rationalized that the story alone was worth the $60 ticket.

Then she smiled at me. You know the kind of smile when someone *really* feels sorry for you. She smiled and handed me yet another ticket for the tow. THAT ticket was another $400!! This day had now cost me over $500 (let's not forget the taxi ride too, where only the jokes were free!) At this point I had officially lost my pleasing personality and I had an old fashion hissy fit. "YOU HAVE GOT TO BE KIDDING ME!" I said. "WHY should I be doubly consequenced? It was only one infraction. I only made ONE mistake. THIS ISN'T FAIR!" I whined. She didn't argue with me. She didn't even offer any further explanations. She simply waited for me to pay. Actually, she said only one thing to me, and I believe it was "I know, sweetie. It really sucks. I bet you won't do that again."

It was only as I was driving home and feeling so frustrated with myself thinking about all the things I could have done with that $500 that it hit me. I realized this is why consequences are so effective. It was because everyone was so kind and compassionate and nobody bothered lecturing or belittling my stupid mistakes that I could actually learn from this experience. And learn I did. You can imagine I will never let that happen again. But what if everyone I had encountered that day had had something to say about my poor choices? What if the cab driver had looked at me with disgust, or the impound lot clerk had started yelling at me when I had my temper tantrum? You can see that my focus on the drive home would have been very different. I would either have focused on feeling ashamed or on the mean people who had made me feel bad. But since neither happened, I could concentrate solely on my behavior. Every person that I came in contact with that day allowed me to simply feel the consequences of the choices I'd made, and thus, I learned my lesson. I will make a very different choice next time I am faced with a similar circumstance.

This is a perfect illustration of what is possible if we, as parents, can step out of the way and let our kids simply experience life's consequences without our emotional reactivity. Of course, I realize that these people I encountered had no emotional connection to me, so letting me feel the consequences without reacting to me was easy. It isn't so easy for parents. Believe me, I get it. But because this is such a clean example of choice and consequence and lessons learned, I think it is a useful illustration. It demonstrates what's possible when emotional reactivity is absent and we can step aside to allow natural and logical consequences to occur. I think of this story often when I am struggling to get out of my children's way and let them learn lessons on their own without my stepping in to soften the blow. It helps.

Teaching Children to Be Responsible Through Choice and Consequence

So by now we have learned that reward and punishment do not teach children how to be responsible, so we should abandon them as discipline strategies. Instead, involving children through choice and consequence is far more effective. Additionally, the key to effective discipline is to establish mutual respect and expect cooperation.

Teaching children that they, not we, are in charge of their lives can't happen early enough. Our children are not our property. We need to help them live their own lives as responsibly as possible. We struggle in this society with a don't-blame-me mentality because from our earliest experiences, we have been taught to rely on others to tell us how to behave. We look to others to reward us when we are good and punish us when we are not. We typically learn this in childhood.

Imagine a world in which we took full personal responsibility for our lives, our choices, and our destinies. That world is possible if we can change the way we raise our children. Giving children choices encourages cooperation and helps them build self-esteem and develop independence. Offering them simple choices respects their desire for control AND your desire to keep order in your home. Set limits, but provide choices within them. Through choices and limit setting, we encourage children to develop internal control.

Examples for Young Children

"This is the last book we'll be reading tonight. Would you like Mommy to read it or Daddy?"
"It's time to get into your pajamas. Do you want the red ones or the blue ones?"
"It's time to put your shoes on. Would you like to wear your boots or your sneakers today?"
"It's time for bed. Would you like to brush your teeth first or use the potty first?

Examples for Adolescents

"You must clean your room this weekend. What time would work best for you?"
"I need to talk with you tonight while you are at your friend's house. Would you like me to call there, or would you prefer to call me? What time would be best for you?"

"I need you to help with chores this weekend. Here is a list of what needs to be done. How would you like to split it up? What time on Sunday would work with your schedule?"

Giving children freedom to choose significantly reduces power struggles. It sends a clear message that you respect them, their needs, and their desire to have a say in their own lives. Remember, children, like adults, don't like to feel controlled. If you can avoid power struggles, you are much more likely to get what you need from your kids.

Keeping emotion—especially anger—out of consequences avoids turning them into punishment. Children are no different from us. We all make choices, and those choices have consequences. If they won't clean up their toys, they can't play with them the next day. Keep it simple; no angry fits or outbursts on your end, just follow-through. Your daughter can't seem to find the time to clean her room? Don't find the time to take her to the mall. Parents have great power. You don't need to yell, scream, hit, or threaten to get your point across. The damage you do to the relationship just isn't worth it. Discipline through choice and consequence, avoids power struggles, and allows choices within limits. These methods will teach your children to behave, build their belief in themselves, and give them a sense of personal responsibility that will last a lifetime.

Saying Yes Instead of No

Learning to say yes instead of no is a powerful parenting strategy. Saying no to your kids sets up a power struggle you are destined to lose. Often it looks something like this: "No, you can't watch TV because you haven't finished your homework." Typically, the child replies, "Yes, I did; most of it anyway. Please,

Mom, just one show." And then you are headed for a long night of frustration and arguments.

Try this instead: "Yes, you can watch TV as soon as your homework is done." Saying yes as often as you can dismantles the power struggle. So instead of, "No, you can't go outside until you clean your room," try "Yes, of course you can go outside, as soon as you clean your room." It's a subtle but important difference. Saying yes changes the whole tone of the conversation. Try it for a day. Say, "Yes, you may, as soon as you _____" instead of "No," and see how it changes the tone of your relationship and creates a newfound spirit of cooperation.

Time-outs, Tantrums, Follow-through, and Payoffs

One of my children (I won't say who) always refused to go into time-out when she was younger. It was mind-numbing. Here I was, parenting coach extraordinaire, and I could not get a four-year-old to accept a time-out. It was embarrassing. One day, in a moment of despair and desperation, I meditated to try to calm down. After meditation, in my now relaxed state, I asked myself, "What would I tell a client who was struggling with this issue?" And then it came to me. This was nothing more than a power struggle. It went something like this: Me: "Go in time-out." Her: "No!" and this went on about a hundred times. Ultimately I would get angry, resulting in the situation shifting from consequence (i.e., natural/logical outcome for a misbehavior) to punishment (i.e., overreaction, hostility, and rage). Additionally, it was clear that my child was getting a payoff. Getting your parents REALLY upset is like hitting the kiddie jackpot! Think about it. Kids have very little control. We tell them what to wear, what to eat, when to eat, how much to eat, where to go, when to go to bed, when to use the toilet, etc. Doesn't it make logical sense that if they can discover the power to get us REALLY angry, they will use it?

When I realized this, the solution became clear. The next time she said "NO!" when asked to go into time-out, can you guess what I said? Here it is: "That's okay, sweetie! No need. Go into time-out whenever you feel ready." Immediately this threw her for a loop. It was not how she had expected the scene to play out. And at that very moment, I got the power back. Much like Dorothy in "The Wizard of Oz," I simply had to remind myself that I'd had the power all along. I didn't need to use my voice or my size to prove it. I just needed to invoke my natural parenting powers. I needed to remember that she was four and I was forty and that all of her wants and desires were supplied by me.

After she was told to go into time-out whenever she felt ready, she began to go about her business as usual. She attempted to watch TV, then to read a book, then to play a game, then to sit down for dinner. The only problem was that she wasn't *allowed* to do any of those things before she sat in her time-out, which I calmly explained to her. She replied "BUT I'M NOT GOING INTO TIME-OUT!!!!!!" I replied "That's okay! You don't need to. But you can't do anything else, including watch TV, read, play a game, or eat dinner until you do." I said this VERY calmly, almost in a singsong fashion, as I was very pleased with myself! When she said, "BUT, I'M HUUUUUUNGRY," I said, "I know, sweetheart, and dinner is not being withheld from you. In fact, I am keeping it warm for you. You may have it as soon as you finish time-out." Eventually, she threw herself into time-out and screamed, "START THE TIMER! I'M IN TIME-OUT!" I calmly explained that the time-out would begin as soon as she stopped screaming, but that she should feel free to scream as long as she felt it was necessary. She screamed for a minute or so, and then, once she was quiet, I started the timer and told her how much time she had before she could join us for dinner.

Rediscovering the power I had in the relationship, and changing my approach as a result, was the tipping point back to a more positive relationship with our daughter. Once we took charge in a real rather than a desperate, frustrated, depleted way, everything shifted.

Kids Don't "Have To" Do Anything, and Neither Do We

Once I accepted that my children didn't *have to* go into time-out, I was ready to take on a broader concept: *You cannot force your children to do anything.* Once you internalize this idea, life gets easier and less confrontational. Our children don't *have to* clean, they don't *have to* speak to us respectfully, or finish their homework, or do their chores, or whatever. *What's important to remember is that they aren't allowed to do anything under our control until they do.* And oh, by the way, we control almost everything if they still live under our roof. This is HUGE! **This concept will change your life.** Simply follow through calmly by saying, "I'm sorry, hon, but I can't take you to Uncle Louie's picnic this evening because you didn't empty the dishwasher as I asked" (or finish your homework, or mow the lawn, or speak to me respectfully, or whatever). Their defiant behavior will stop as soon as you can manage your anxiety about their missing Uncle Louie's family picnic.

Not easy, is it? They are counting on the fact that you can't manage your feelings of embarrassment or disappointment. Or maybe you can't handle that your *child* will be disappointed. Or worse yet, your child may disappoint Uncle Louie. I promise you, Uncle Louie will recover! The question is, will you? Is it more important to miss the picnic (or baseball practice, or guitar lessons, or ballet class, etc.) or to teach your child that you mean what you say and follow through with consequences? Remember, and remind your child, that missing the picnic was HIS choice when he decided to behave inappropriately. He will get another chance next time. If you can follow through calmly with consequences, there are likely to be very few "next times."

For this parenting skill to be effective, you also need to be okay with the fact that your child is going to push back. He is not going to say, "Sounds like a great parenting approach, Ma. I am lucky to have you." He is going to be angry, and he will let you know it in every way he can. Whatever. Expect it, emotionally prepare for it, and then ignore it. If you can't ignore it, go take a bath.

Respect ≠ Fear

Respect is created by clear limit-setting and consistently following through without anger or violence. It is critical that your children feel free to make their own mistakes without fearing your reactions. **Never, under any circumstance, strike a child.** Spanking (definition: hitting a child in any way, which includes, but is not limited to, a swat on the butt, slapping hands, pinching, slapping a face, etc.) has been scientifically proven in research studies over and over to create anger and aggression in children. Often these children become angry, hostile, or depressed adults.

Whenever I see anyone hitting a child, I call the police. It's an act of violence. It's barbaric. Yet many people still see spanking or striking a child as an acceptable form of discipline. But think about it. If you saw a man strike a woman, you wouldn't call it discipline. You'd call it assault, which it is. And it's illegal, as it should be. Now consider the size and strength difference between an adult and a child. No one is more helpless than a child, yet they get the least protection from society. Why isn't hitting a child also considered assault? I don't understand how this behavior can continue in our society and still be socially acceptable and legal. Nothing kills a child's spirit faster than being intimidated physically by an adult who says he loves him, but who is purposely trying to physically hurt and/or intimidate him. The brain simply can't make sense of the contradiction. Please. Don't. Spanking may stop an unwanted behavior quickly, but at a HUGE cost. It creates a relationship based on fear rather than love and respect. If you choose to spank your child, please know that you will teach him absolutely nothing— except to hit someone smaller than he is when he finds their behavior unacceptable. Children who are spanked are often bullies in training. Spanking encourages rebellion, creates shame, and humiliates children. Additionally, no matter what some may tell you, parents DO spank out of frustration and anger, and it hurts. Do we want to hurt our children? I pray the answer is NO.

As parents, we want our children to respect us, not fear us. Often I see parents get these two concepts confused. Fear teaches nothing, but it does create distance, discomfort, and a feeling of being unsafe in the relationship. To build RESPECT, simply decide on a few rules and determine what the consequences will be if those rules aren't followed. If the rules are broken, follow through with the predetermined consequence in a calm, matter-of-fact way EVERY TIME. You get respect by giving respect and exercising your parental power in appropriate, loving ways, and you teach your child the art of self-control at the same time. When you practice restraint, your children learn restraint.

Respect is earned. We cannot demand that our children respect us simply because we scream at them and demand it. Respect is earned by showing them that we mean what we say and say what we mean. We follow through on consequences, we don't lose control, and we role model the respectful behavior we expect from them.

New Rule

I am about to give you two of the most powerful words in the English language. You have the power to change any unwanted behavior in your home just by stating these two words: NEW RULE. It's that simple. "Hey, new rule everyone: TV is limited to one hour a day." "Hey guys, new rule: we only touch each other if we are giving hugs or handshakes. No more wrestling." "This just in, new rule: we do homework after school, not after dinner." "New rule: WE ALL help clean up after a meal." I think you get the idea. Often parents think that since they've allowed an unwanted behavior to go on for so long, it's too late. It's like that old saying "You can't teach an old dog new tricks." Not true! First, you *can* teach an old dog new tricks, AND you can teach any child—even adult children—that the rules have changed regardless of how long the unwanted behavior has been occurring. It's done by changing the rules, stating them clearly, and following through with consequences one hundred percent of the time when the rules aren't followed.

Here's an example of a new rule that I instituted when I grew tired of fighting with my kids about electronics. I simply said, "New rule: no TV/computer on Wednesdays." Having a whole day without electronics simplified the issue. It's so quiet and lovely at my house on Wednesdays! This rule is straightforward and it works. But the key was following through every Wednesday without exception. What if the kids "forget" and my husband or I come home to find them watching TV on a Wednesday? "That's okay;" it's no TV/computer Thursday this week.

Speaking of electronics, here's another new rule challenge: change the rules in your house for two weeks to include only thirty minutes of technology three days a week, one hour of technology each day on the weekends, and two days of NO technology at all. Let the kids choose which days, but make them the same two days both weeks. After the initial balking, you will be pleasantly surprised at how many behavior issues disappear. After just two days of doing this new routine in my house, I could not believe how enjoyable it was to be with my family. The children had the time and space to connect with us more, they got really creative with their down time, and they spent more one-on-one time with friends and each other. It was downright delightful! We liked it so much that it's now our new permanent limit for technology. Don't take my word for how big an impact it makes; try it for yourself for two weeks! What do you have to lose?

Rules are Rules

Remember that whatever family rules and norms you establish remain true no matter where you are or with whom you spend your time. It is confusing to your child if certain rules apply only at home and not elsewhere or with other people in charge. Often rules change outside of the home because enforcing the rules in public raises our anxiety. We fear the judgment and criticism of others. Our children can "smell the fear," and they'll see its presence as a perfect opportunity to act out. Don't blame them; that is just how they're built. Instead, work on managing *your* anxiety so you offer the same choices and follow through with the same consequences at home and away. It won't take long for the kids to figure out that they don't have the option of getting away with unacceptable behavior outside the home.

In addition, teach your babysitters and other caregivers the family rules. Sit down with them and discuss your parenting rules. Provide examples of how you would handle certain misbehaviors. It isn't disrespectful to share this information. In fact, it is incredibly helpful for the caregivers, and absolutely essential for your child's well-being.

Consistency is Key

Be consistent with the messages you send. For example, I hear some parents say they allow their children to drink alcohol or smoke marijuana at home because they believe that if the behavior is permitted at home, the kids won't need to experiment outside, where the parents cannot supervise or control it. This is CRAZY thinking! By allowing your child to smoke and drink in your home, the clear message you send is, "I'm okay with this behavior." You are letting your child know that she has your permission and your blessing to engage in the very behavior you are trying to discourage. Remember, it is what you DO, not what you SAY that is internalized by your child. Your being permissive in this way sends a strong and clear message that it's okay with you. If that is the intended message, fine. But don't fool yourself into thinking that you are sending a message that will discourage these behaviors.

Chapter Six Take-away

Children need rules, limits, and discipline, but they must be free to make choices within those limits. Set limits, but give your children options so they don't feel controlled, trapped, or frustrated.

seven

Managing Unwanted Behavior: Teach the Art of Self-Discipline

I think of discipline as the continual everyday process
of helping a child learn self-discipline.

~ *Fred Rogers*

Our main job as parents as it relates to discipline is to teach our children to manage themselves when we are not present. Our hope is that our children make sound, healthy choices from a place of self-worth and internal clarity and calm. We hope that their life choices come from an intrinsic sense of self that they develop over time. We want them to make healthy choices because they know that these choices are best for them, and because they know they deserve to live a happy, healthy, and safe life. We don't want them to make choices based on fear, insecurity, a need for external validation, or anticipated disapproval. We want choices to come from their own inner voices.

We can help them develop this grounding. This chapter explains how. The key, of course, is managing yourself.

Hold the Line

It is your job to hold the line and your children's job to push against it. If you can accept this truth, you can stop being so angry with them. It is totally appropriate for your children to test every limit you set. That's the whole point of childhood. Why do we get angry when they are just doing what they were born to do? My theory: because we struggle with the anxiety that comes from trying to hold the line. They are good at their job (testing), but we're not so great at ours (holding). So we get angry with them for showing us our weaknesses and vulnerabilities. It's like we are thinking, "If you would just stop testing me, then I wouldn't have to feel so inadequate."

However, if we can begin to think about our children as being here to teach US *about ourselves rather than the other way around, we will start heading in the right direction.* Allow your kids to show you, through testing limits, what in **you** needs attention and healing. As I've mentioned, for me, it's patience. Perhaps for you, it's a tendency to judge, or perfectionism, or poor self-control. Changing the way you think about your kids testing limits from you teaching them to them teaching you will go a long way toward healing yourself, your family, and ultimately the world. No pressure. ☺

Ignoring Unwanted Behavior

Having a child who doesn't like something and speaks negatively about it constantly (e.g., school, dinner, siblings, life in general), can be frustrating and disheartening. If your child is behaving in this way, I suggest you take a calm, neutral approach. Try ignoring this behavior. I mean really ignoring it. Not just today, but every day. And not just by not verbally responding. No eye rolling, sighing, expressive body language, or anything else you do to communicate your discontent. Behaviors only continue when there is a payoff. And the payoff in your child's case is your reaction, whether it's negative or positive. It doesn't matter; it's all for the attention. If there is no payoff, the behavior will cease. That's just basic psychology. That said, sometimes we simply can't stand to hear one more negative comment. When that moment hits, I calmly create a new rule. I might do something like this: "Hey guys, new rule: no complaining about dinner. The next person who complains about dinner will have to sit on the step without dinner until we finish eating. And yes, you will still have to clean up."

Handling Back Talk

I get a lot of questions about how to handle a kid who backtalks. I am never sure exactly what this means as every parent has different definitions and tolerances for this type of behavior. If your child is upset, angry, or disagrees with you, so what? This is America. Isn't that allowed? If your child is making fun of you when you ask him to do something, simply give him a consequence. If your child is cursing at you or engaging in potty talk, he gets a consequence for that too, but a bigger one. In either case, be sure that you have defined clear rules ahead of time, and be sure you're not engaging in the behavior too. Otherwise, you send a mixed message.

When setting rules, be careful. If you have too many rules, like they aren't allowed to express a feeling or an opinion different from yours, you are just inviting trouble. Kids need to have the freedom to talk. You will need to manage yourself, not them. If they aren't doing what you've asked, then give them a consequence—immediately, and without anger. Stop yelling and don't engage with them. That's where they are learning that behavior. If they are doing what you asked but simply expressing an opinion that they aren't happy about it, let it go.

I HATE You

If you are parenting really well, at some point your child will say those dreaded words "I HATE YOU." "That's okay." He doesn't, really. But he feels like he does at the moment, and that needs to be okay too. Your child knows you better than ANYONE, and he knows just what to say to get your attention and push your buttons. If you want to hear the button-pushing declaration many more times, give it lots of attention. If you don't, acknowledge it and move on. "I'm sorry to hear that, sweetie. I love you very much. What are you in the mood to eat for dinner, hon?" Do not respond to whatever it is he says next. Typically, it's "NO YOU DON'T. YOU HATE ME. YOU'VE ALWAYS HATED ME," etc., etc., and blah blah blah. Ignore it. Go someplace or call someone who will appreciate and support you and give you a round of applause. Because what most likely caused this explosion was your ability to make a tough parenting decision, stick to your position, and manage your anxiety, to which your child is now reacting. Good for you! Keep it up.

Overcoming Myths and Stereotypes

There are certain myths about children that get us into trouble. If we believe that a certain stage in a child's life means that this or that bad thing *has* to happen, or a certain type of child will *always* behave in such-and-such a negative way, we render ourselves powerless to deal with our children as the individuals they are. Don't give in to these generalizations. A myth is a story, not a fact. Your child is who he or she is, not a category. Let me explain.

When I hear the saying *boys will be boys*, the little hairs on the back of my neck stand up. What does this mean? Does it imply that boys are beasts by birth and we can't possibly expect them to manage their savage impulses? While it is true that most boys have more testosterone than girls, it is also true that the majority of their aggressive behavior is a direct result of poor limit-setting by caregivers. Boys CAN manage their behavior when they are expected to, as can girls. Parents who believe the boys-will-be-boys way of thinking often permit—dare I say, encourage—rough-housing, wrestling, playing with guns, and playing violent video games. By permitting these behaviors, you encourage them. The same parents who permit these behaviors are then surprised when their children get into trouble at school for fighting. They shouldn't be surprised; they set that up.

Similarly, I often hear, "You know how girls can be, right?" I believe those who say this are referring to the catty behavior girls sometimes exhibit in their childhood friendships. Girls are not catty by nature. Often boys get the reputation for being physically aggressive, while girls get a reputation for being relationally aggressive. You know what I mean—the "I am not going to be your best friend anymore unless you invite me to your birthday party" kind of stuff. This behavior should not be tolerated as "age-appropriate," nor should you assume that it will pass. It needs to stop immediately. Girls (and boys) need constant redirection that reminds them that their words can be hurtful. They need to develop appropriate skills to manage relationships. Don't blow off catty behavior as no big deal, because it is a big deal! If the behavior continues despite redirection, then institute consequences every time your children use their words and friendships as weapons. Remember—no anger, no hostility, just peaceful consequences. *You can only teach peace by being peaceful.*

There are certain parenting myths that were started long ago and have been repeated so many times that people have accepted them as truths. One of these myths is that adolescence is AWFUL. Honestly, it doesn't need to be that way—at least not on the parenting side of the equation. It is a sensitive time, for sure. There is a lot going on. But if you have been managing your anxiety, giving choices and consequences without anger, and allowing your children to take personal responsibility for their actions, you'll be fine. You may take more baths than before, but what's wrong with that? Enjoy EVERY stage of your child's life. Adolescence is no exception. Just set limits, keep the rules and boundaries clear, and make the most of this time together.

Another popular myth is the "terrible twos." Ironically, adolescence and toddlerhood are parallel processes. If you think about it, these two stages have identical goals. The child (or adolescent) is trying to assert himself and beginning to differentiate from the parent. So the toddler says "Do it MYSELF!" and the adolescent says, "Leave me alone!" Either way, take the hint. Let him work out his struggles on his own.

I often tell parents that toddlers who are potty training are really training the parents. They are trying to teach us that we can't MAKE THEM do anything. They will poop in the toilet when they are ready and not a second before. It is absolutely fine to encourage them to use the potty, but it is CRAZY to force them or punish them when they don't. If we can internalize the message that they are in charge of their own bodies, their own choices, and their own lives, parenting becomes easier. Back off. Go to the movies, or better yet, go take a bath. And remember that your child is an individual, not a member of a category who is predestined to behave in a particular way.

The "Lazy" Child

There is no such thing as a "lazy" child. Parents often use this term to describe a hard-to-motivate child, but the reality is that unmotivated children are simply uninspired. You will be AMAZED at how motivated they become when they *are* inspired. One way you can motivate or inspire them is to hold back something important to them until they do what you have asked. Example: "I noticed you didn't take out the trash, empty the dishwasher, or mow the lawn like I asked you. 'That's okay.' Do it whenever. Just let me know when you feel like doing it, and I will be happy to take you to that party, baseball game, mall, friend's house."

A child also becomes inspired when he finds something he LOVES. Help him discover what that might be by removing all the cluttering activities that distract him from finding it (TV, video games, etc.). "Unmotivated" and "lazy" are also terms used to describe children who may actually be depressed. If you feel this may be the issue, seek professional attention immediately.

"Come Here, Sweet Cheeks"

When I am still in control but on the verge of losing patience with my children, I bring myself back from the brink by ending my requests with an endearing term of the day. My personal favorite, most fun, and most recent discovery, thanks to my friend Pat Rayno, is "doll." "I asked you five times to empty the dishwasher, doll." It may sound silly, but using this kind of endearment works. It reminds us that the person we are angry with, and with whom we are about to lose control, is also our precious, dearest loved one. "I just tripped over your shoes, which are in the middle of the floor, hon. Can you pick them up now, sweetheart?" The trick here is not to sound sarcastic, which is my personal challenge.

I find it fun to discover new, endearing terms. I can keep myself entertained all day long with my own self-imposed parenting challenges. Some days I laugh at myself more than others. I encourage you to try this technique as a means of managing anxiety by resisting the urge to scream. Losing control won't get the job done, or if it does, it's not without cost to the relationship. Instead, "Sweetie, I noticed you're not eating. Please stop distracting your brother who is, honey. No worries; you can eat tomorrow, shmoops. Thanks for listening, doll!"

Write a Note

Sometimes it is nearly impossible to ask your child to do something without experiencing great frustration or anger. "That's okay;" you're only human. At that moment, simply write a note instead of talking to him. You can write what you cannot say without sounding irritated. So instead of saying, "If I ask you ONE MORE TIME to clean your room, you will NOT be going to softball practice tonight," you can write, "Dear Nick, I noticed your room still isn't clean. We will leave for softball practice as soon as it's done. Have a great day! Love you, Mom."

Sleep in Your Own Bed

When your toddler refuses to sleep in his own bed and you have been up all night fighting with him, you may feel like there is no hope. Oh, there's hope! This situation is no different from any other power struggle you may encounter. Let your toddler know that if he chooses to sleep in your bed tonight, "that's okay," but he is also choosing to _____ (fill in the blank with something very important to him). Perhaps he won't be going to a birthday party he was looking forward to, or he won't be allowed to watch his favorite program, or have his favorite dessert, or favorite toy, etc. The consequence chosen only lasts until bedtime the following day.

Remember, if you can tolerate your anxiety and have patience, you are set for life! You are teaching your child at the earliest age that he gets to choose his path, but that there are consequences to his choices. Gently remind him the following evening that he gets another chance to make a different choice. Remind him what his consequence was today and what it will be tomorrow if he chooses to sleep with you. But most important, let him know it is HIS CHOICE. Remain calm and nonchalant. If he senses that you have an agenda or that there is a "wrong" choice to make, it won't work. Either choice has to be okay. If you do this well, he will be sleeping in his own bed within three days.

Fun with Discipline

Are you tired of the kids fighting in the backseat of the car? Try this approach: say nothing! (That'll get their attention). Pull over as soon as it is safe to do so. Take out a book, magazine, or old newspaper that you have stashed under the driver's seat for this purpose. Start reading. Stay totally silent. When the kids ask why you have stopped, simply ask, in the calmest and least sarcastic voice you have, "Are you done fighting?" Once they are quiet, resume driving. Works one hundred percent of the time! (And super fun too). If you have VERY stubborn kids, you may have to find a park so you can actually get out of the car and read on a bench. The average time to stop sibling fighting with this approach is somewhere between fifteen seconds and two minutes. Yes, it will be inconvenient, and you may be late for something, but if you do this a few times consistently, you will abolish fighting in the backseat forever. I promise it's worth the inconvenience. It's short-term pain for a lifetime gain!

It's Not Personal, Might as Well Laugh About It

Don't take it all so personally. If your child is being snotty, obnoxious, ungrateful, rude, and all-around nasty, chances are it's not about you. Growing up is really hard. Have you forgotten? And who better to unload on than the people you know will never ever leave you or stop loving you. If you can manage it, say "Sounds like you need a hug." If you can't, walk away and go take a bath. If you MUST say or do something, let her know what you won't be doing for her if the tone of disrespect continues, then for the love of Pete, just follow through. Don't say another word about it. In these moments, I suggest you call the funniest friend you have and ask her to reframe the story into something you can laugh about.

Chapter Seven Take-away

Don't get upset with your children for doing what children are supposed to do: test limits. Hold the line, and don't let their irritating behavior get to you. Remain calm, and learn from them. Perhaps their actions are showing you that there's some work *you* need to do on your own anxieties and vulnerabilities. Do it.

eight
Back to Basics:
Simplicity As a Path to
Wholeness

Be content with what you have, rejoice in the way things are. When you realize there is nothing lacking, the whole world belongs to you.

~ Lao Tzu

Just as society struggles with a perpetual compulsion to acquire more and more, our kids, too, are drowning in a desire for "stuff." We keep working harder to obtain more things that we don't really need, and when we get them, we feel unfulfilled and start all over again. It's a crazy, never-ending treadmill. However, the more evolved a person is, the more she understands that real joy is found in keeping life simple. We don't realize it, but this endless desire to collect more stuff is another manifestation of our unresolved issues unconsciously playing out in our parenting. We don't recognize that through our own chronic consumption, we are communicating a toxic message of "need more stuff" to our children. And it's not just about the stuff. It's also about the constant need to perform, academically or otherwise. We don't need to do that either. Let's stop the insanity and get back to what yields true happiness: love, limits, and simple pleasures.

When is Enough Enough?

If you want to teach your children the art of appreciation, stop giving them so much! Gratitude and appreciation come from having something special once in a while. How can we expect our kids to appreciate a vacation if we go away every month? How can we expect gratitude over the shirt we bought them at the mall today if we just went clothes shopping last week? Just because your children may have been born into a privileged household where food is plentiful and the house is bigger than they need, doesn't mean they get stuff just because you can afford it. In fact, if you can afford it, I would double your efforts to hold back.

Often when a family is on a very limited income, the child gets few treats, so feeling gratitude and appreciation comes more easily, as was the case for me growing up. Make sure your kids know to expect very little. And that lesson doesn't come from a conversation. It comes from a life experience of getting very little. If they ask you for something at the mall say, "Oh, is it your birthday?" Our children are entitled to love, respect, food, shelter, health care, basic clothing, and school supplies. That's it. Everything else is a treat, a gift, a once-in-a-while, special occasion kind of thing. If you can do this, I promise you that your kids will learn to appreciate the treats that come their way occasionally. If you can't resist, then it isn't your kids who have the issue.

Limits!

Limits are wonderful. Limit your child's sugar intake. Limit video games. Limit TV. Limit after-school activities. Limit everything! Let your children know that boundaries exist and boundaries are GOOD. Limits are what keep us sane in this topsy-turvy world. We struggle to limit our own food intake, alcohol consumption, and work hours. S L O W down. Take a breath and allow yourself to accept the limit without allowing your brain to send a message of deprivation. Limits do not equal deprivation. Limits equal sanity, balance, and peace.

Stop Buying "Stuff"!

When your children have too much "stuff," it is hard to teach them the source of real happiness. The stuff is incredibly distracting from what brings true joy. What we all long for is connection, love, friendship, laughter, and time spent together. What we really need is to know that we matter to one another and that what we feel is heard and cared about by those we love the most. You can enjoy your friends on the back deck just as easily as you can on an expensive vacation. When your phone, Facebook, or video games are constantly distracting you, you cannot listen or be listened to. It takes courage to walk away from the stuff and just be with one another. But that's where the fruit is, my friend. I promise. Why not encourage your children through role modeling to take a break from all the stuff and simply be?

Choose a New Approach to School

Work at nurturing a child who is kind and compassionate rather than a child who is focused on overachieving in academic pursuits. Balance is the key to life. Too much pressure on grades and performance can create perfectionism and anxiety. Instead, focus on teaching your child the art of self-care, friendship, compassion, kindness, and FUN. Those are the skills most needed to succeed in life anyway. A child who is riddled with anxiety because she feels she has to live up to external expectations of academic excellence is not a child who will grow up happy or self-confident.

Many parents get caught up in the race to the top—signing their children up for advanced classes because they believe they are "better" for them. And maybe they are. That's a personal choice for you and your child to make (but mostly your child). However, I would suggest that when making that choice, you consider the long-term consequences, both good and bad, and make the choice *consciously*. In my practice, I have seen many kids self-destruct from the pressures of trying to keep up, be the best, and race to stay ahead of their peers. Not everyone can be at the top of a gifted class. If you are a parent who demands per-fection, be prepared for some profound hits to your child's sense of self-worth. If your kid *is* one of those few at the top, you need to ensure that high achievement doesn't lead to perfectionism, as perfectionism has serious consequences as well. Think about this issue seriously before you and your child choose the path of accelerated classes. As Albert Einstein said, "Everyone is a genius. But if you judge a fish on its ability to climb a tree, it will live its whole life believing it is stupid."

Freedom

Hopscotch. Wire ball. Kickball. Tag. When I was growing up, parents would say, "Come in when it gets dark." Remember those days? Can we get back to them? Even a little? I know families who allow *no* electronics except for a few select programs on TV. They understand and grasp the idea of simple pastimes. They allow their kids to roam the neighborhood, trusting that they're okay. Those kids are doing pretty well. And the reality is that the incidence of horrible things happening to our children is really no different from in the past. What has changed is the twenty-four-hour news cycle that makes these rare incidents look common. Vivid images are replayed over and over again, giving us the false impression that there is far more evil than good in the world and thus, we must overprotect our children. These stories are disturbing and serve no purpose but to exacerbate our parental anxiety. Try to keep the anxiety at bay and allow your children the freedom to enjoy playtime and the fresh air they need. Teach them that the world is a safe, beautiful place. If you don't, you are assisting in setting them up for a lifetime of fear and anxiety.

Facebook (and Instagram, and Twitter...)

Families experience all kinds of issues that arise from social media. When I suggest that maybe social media shouldn't be permitted, some parents look at me like I've just asked them to sacrifice their first-born. It really is okay to say no to your child even if "everyone else is doing it."

I have made it clear to my children that they will never have a Facebook account as long as they live in my house. Facebook is a breeding ground for inappropriate language, behavior, and bullying. Parents are just asking for trouble by allowing kids under eighteen to go onto the site.

Social relationships are a beautiful yet stressful and challenging training ground for life. It's tough to look someone in the eyes and speak cruelly about them, but it can feel easier to type out cruel comments on Facebook in the heat of confusing feelings. Kids are struggling to learn how to navigate personal relationships. Relationships, even the healthiest ones—*especially* the healthiest ones—are very hard work! Facebook makes friendship look easy. This isn't an honest message to send. I'm sorry, but you don't have 487 "friends." We are blessed if we have three.

Childhood is a vulnerable time, and we have so little time to teach our kids how to manage budding relationships and all that is involved in being a good friend. To be a good friend requires conflict resolution and listening skills, loving support and encouragement, and knowing how to approach sensitive subjects that can lead to difficult conversations with people you love. Friendship is an art form, a skill that takes a lifetime to develop. Facebook is a distraction from all that.

At a minimum, if you aren't able to, or don't feel it's necessary to say no, you need to monitor your child's involvement very closely. I strongly encourage parents to have the computer in plain sight so they can easily see what their kids are doing and saying, and what they are being exposed to. Make sure you have their passwords so you can periodically check their activity. Children tend to keep their interactions more appropriate when they know that their parents can check on them without notice. Same rules apply for texting.

UNPLUG!

When kids unplug from technology, a miracle occurs. To clarify, by technology I mean anything with a plug or a battery, so that includes TV. The miracle is that the neurons in your children's brains have to work to find something else to do. Initially, when they withdraw, it's a little like watching an alcoholic or heroin addict detox. It's unpleasant. But just as with any other addiction, a beautiful life with endless possibilities awaits on the other side.

By now you know that the hardest part is managing your anxiety. Can you stand by and watch the detox without jumping in (or rather, giving in) by supplying more of the drug? If your child can use technology socially, create a structure for her to use it. Perhaps you can limit her involvement to a certain number of hours per day or decide on a specific time at night when the cell phone and/or the TV is turned off. Maybe use family vacations as temporary cold turkey opportunities to prevent distractions during family time. If your child is so far into technology that she has become addicted to electronics, sobriety is the only way to go. Just cut it all off cold turkey. You will need to decide where your child stands on this continuum and act accordingly.

Simplify

It is not our job to rush around driving our kids from one activity to the next. It is our job to teach them to be happy with less. We want to teach them *limits* and about choosing what's most important to them. When your children come to you asking to participate in four different activities after school, respond by asking them to think about what interests them the most and choose based on their prioritized list. If they can't decide, suggest they select an activity they'd like to commit to this year and one they'd like to try next year. If this feels too rigid for your family, how about picking one activity from September to December and another activity from January to June?

By asking your children to choose, you are teaching them many important life skills. First, you will help them focus on one interest at a time, which is really important to maintain their sanity. It is impossible to give your full commitment and attention to four activities at once, and it creates stress and anxiety in the child when he feels he is expected to do so. It also creates stress in the whole family system as you are racing through dinner to get your child to the next activity.

You are also helping your child learn to make decisions, prioritize, and set limits. Limit-setting is a form of self-discipline, which we already know is critical to a child's development. And, of course, my personal favorite is that you are teaching your child that *your* time also matters. You have a life too, remember? And as you are busy making your own life a priority, there is no time to be spending every night taxiing your child to her many activities. It is far more critical to her upbringing to show her that *your* priorities are also important. And by this stage of the book, I hope your priorities include a whole lot of being still, along with regularly scheduled date nights, routine nights out with friends, and quiet nights at home to enjoy your long, luxurious bubble baths! This demonstration of self-care is far more important than chauffeuring your children around town so they can indulge every new interest they decide they'd like to pursue. They have a whole lifetime to explore their interests, one at a time. As we begin to clear up the conflict and chaos in the schedule, we begin to clear out the conflict and chaos in ourselves. This process of "cleaning house" starts in the home, spreads to our community, and eventually our world becomes one of calm and serenity.

Create Simple Memories

It is so easy to get caught up in the day-to-day, mundane, nitty-gritty aspects of parenting. Before you know it, the day is gone, the month has passed, and another year is behind you. Suddenly, you find yourself with an eighteen-year-old and wonder where the time went. I strongly encourage you to CREATE simple memories for your family. Deliberately plan joyous moments, or at the very least, opportunities for them to spontaneously appear. Decide that you will take time EACH DAY to consciously choose to enjoy parenting. This simple but effective change will impact your life (and the lives of your children) in a powerfully positive way. Try it! Making a choice to enjoy our children is a deliberate action we must take. It doesn't always occur automatically, especially when we are going through rough patches.

Chapter Eight Take-away

Get back to the basics; the simple pleasures are the most enjoyable and lead to contentment and peace. Focus on role modeling the simple life and encourage the same in your children.

nine

Extraordinary Parenting: Strategies, Skills, and Tips

If you want children to keep their feet on the ground,
put some responsibility on their shoulders.
~ Abigail Van Buren

Cesar Milan, the Dog Whisperer, says, "I rehabilitate dogs; I train people." I would say, "I rehabilitate kids; I train parents." It is almost always the parents who most need to change, not the child. This doesn't necessarily mean that parents are doing anything wrong per se, but often they insist on using a strategy that doesn't work for the child they actually have as opposed to the child they had envisioned. It is the parents who need the training to stretch out of their view of what *should* work and begin to focus on what *will* work. It sounds simple enough: if it isn't working, stop doing it. Yet often parents continue the same strategy despite overwhelming evidence that it is not working.

This chapter contains strategies, skills, and tips I have found to be helpful for most families. I offer these suggestions as alternatives to the strategies you may be using that seem reasonable but simply aren't working. I trust that these parenting tips will make your life a whole lot happier.

Make Friends With Feelings

There are no "bad" emotions. Sadness, disappointment, frustration, and anger are all part of the human experience. Embrace them. Don't wish your feelings away. Make friends with them. Welcome them. They are fleeting, temporary. The only two feelings to be avoided are shame and guilt, although they too are part of the human experience. Avoid shaming your children; don't overreact to their struggles, lack of skills, mistakes, or bad moods. Work at keeping a neutral stance as they express their emotions. Their behavior may be unpleasant to watch. It may make you anxious. But piling on your reactions to their experiences confuses and escalates the situation. If you do that, they will lose sight of which feelings are theirs and which are yours. Stay out of their way and remind them that this experience will soon be in the past. Remember, everything, including how they are feeling in the moment, is temporary.

Choose Encouragement Over Criticism

Sometimes it feels so hard to find anything worth encouraging when your child is going through a rough stage. Dig deeper. There is always *something* you can encourage. "Johnny, thanks so much for showering today." Find SOMETHING—ANYTHING! Then really and truly shine the light there. "Oh, you smell so good!" "I just love it when you remember to brush your teeth!"

I promise that the more you focus on what's working, the more that behavior and other great behaviors like it will show up. And we all feel better when encouraging words, spoken with genuine feeling, fill the air.

I once watched Deepak Chopra being interviewed on an Oprah show. At one point during the interview, Mr. Chopra shared the fact that his son often got into trouble during math class. He hated math and so he chose to doodle cartoons instead of paying attention. His wife was concerned about this behavior. But Mr. Chopra said he trusted that his son would someday be a cartoon artist and hire an accountant to handle the math. And that's exactly what happened!

As parents, we get so worked up when our kids aren't excelling in EVERYTHING. Guess what? They're not going to be good at EVERYTHING. Are you? Focus on the strengths and abilities that are unique to them. We all have these. Help them to feel proud of the gifts they DO have, and trust they will compensate for the skills they DON'T have. By focusing on their strengths, we help build their self-confidence rather than feeding into their feelings of inadequacy.

Make a commitment today to say only encouraging words to your kids. Resist the urge to redirect, criticize, or offer suggestions about how they can do things differently. This is a great exercise in consciousness. By making a silent commitment to offer only loving and encouraging comments, you will become acutely aware of how often you say things that may be interpreted by your child as critical. Try it for a day and see what new level of awareness you can achieve. As my daughter said to me recently in response to some unsolicited feedback I was offering, "Let's snuggle. More loving, less tips." I think that says it all.

Build Trust

When your child confesses that she did something awful (either out of guilt or duress), take a deep breath and say, "Thank you for telling me." Then walk away—slowly. By doing this, you accomplish two things. First and most important, you preserve the relationship. What your child will remember most from the experience is that she can tell you anything, and that above all, honesty is what is valued most in your family. Second, by walking away, you have a chance to process what you've just heard, manage anxiety, and consciously CHOOSE how you'd like to proceed. If you don't do this, you will be likely to react unconsciously. By reacting emotionally/unconsciously, you run the risk of shaming a child who has simply made a poor choice from which she needs to learn. Your emotional response will cause damage to your relationship and prevent your child from learning a better way. Remember, nothing can be taught or learned in an anxious environment. By choosing your response consciously, you will nurture your relationship AND help your child learn from her choices. Win-win!

Don't Take the Bait

Sometimes our children will ask for our feedback on an issue. It may even be an adult child who asks. And boy, are we thrilled! Finally, an invitation to share our opinions about what our child should or shouldn't do. However, the truth is, most of the time, he doesn't REALLY want to hear our feedback. I know he asked, but watch out—it's a trap! If you answer, he may attack.

I've found the best course of action is to stop and take a breath. After a pause, ask your child if he really wants your feedback. Taking a moment's pause may be enough to snap him back to a truthful answer, which is often NO! However, if he really does want your feedback, ask a lot of questions rather than giving in to the impulse to tell him what to do. By asking questions you help him figure out what *he* wants to do. Yes, this is yet another exercise in anxiety management.

Be You!

Never persuade your child to water down his personality so that he can be more pleasing to others (friends, family, the community), or to avoid teasing or bullying. Your child is a perfect child of God who *doesn't need to change anything* about who he is. He may need to learn some coping mechanisms or manners, but his basic self is just fine. If you find that your child has some quirky parts of his personality that make him vulnerable to teasing by others, teach him the absolute truth—that the person doing the teasing has the problem, not him. No message should include having to change one's personality in order to avoid teasing. If you advise him to change in this way, you send a clear message that even YOU think there is something wrong with your child. And that is a very dangerous message indeed.

If your child is being bullied and you feel he is in danger, intervene immediately. If the situation is not drastic, help him learn how to manage himself in these difficult situations. Encourage kind behavior *from him* even when the other person is not being kind *to him*. Many parents are great at teaching their children how to share or to be kind to those who do the same. But what if we started to teach and role model the idea that we can be kind to others even if they aren't kind to us? This simple approach alone could completely turn the world around.

I once worked with a colleague who truly COULD NOT stand me. I don't know why; I'm delightful ☺. But regardless of my winning personality, this person did not enjoy me one bit. Every day I had to see him, work with him, and interact with him. Although being rude to him certainly felt justified, it felt so wrong on a cellular level. Instead, I chose to smile a lot. I truly tried to kill him with kindness! While he probably didn't like me any better as a result, he certainly kept his behavior on the up and up. The truth is, it is almost impossible to be mean to someone who is being nice to you. This skill will carry your child far! Try it yourself, too. See what a difference it makes in your day.

We Are More Alike Than Different

When you teach love, compassion, tolerance, acceptance, and celebrating the joy of our differences, you give your child the tools for a life of peace. We may not always agree with each other. People will come into our lives and they will look, speak, and sound unlike anyone we have ever met. "That's okay!" Actually, that's cool. The truth is that we are far more similar than we are different. We all want to be loved, accepted, and understood. We want to know that what we feel matters. Encourage your child to be curious about differences instead of feeling threatened by them. This cannot happen, of course, unless you role model the same.

Discussing Sensitive Topics

What do you do when your child asks questions about those tough situations in life? Often, in an effort to protect children from hurt or worry, parents limit the information they reveal about difficult topics such as the illness of a family member, impending separation, financial struggles, etc. However, our children usually know much more than we think. In fact, when we withhold information, they create a scenario in their own minds that is often far worse than the truth.

I strongly encourage you to let your kids in on what is going on in the family—at an age-appropriate level. By telling them the truth, you help them manage their anxiety and you create an environment that builds trust and encourages questions. When your children ask questions, you begin to discover what they are thinking, and that lets you help them sort out difficult feelings. Furthermore, it's okay that if by talking about these topics with them, you experience your own challenging feelings at the same time. It's helpful for our kids to see us as feeling beings; doing so allows us to go through difficult times together, which brings us closer to one another.

Relationship Skills

Cultivating and maintaining friendships over a lifetime is one of the most fulfilling and difficult challenges we face. Oh, how I wish there were a Friendship 101 class in school to teach us how to have difficult conversations, agree to disagree when necessary, support one another in good times and bad, and stay the course even when things get rocky. Relationships of all types are very hard, and this fact isn't talked about nearly enough. So when things get tough, we assume it's time to run screaming for the hills.

I'm as guilty as the next person. But I can honestly say from personal experience that it's worth it to stick it out. Teach your children the art of friendship. Predict for them the rocky parts that are inevitable in any worthwhile relationship. Teach them that when times get tough, it's an amazing opportunity for them to shine. Teach them the skills required to weather the storm. These skills include compromise, honesty, and a willingness to see another person's perspective. Relationship skills are required for a fulfilling life, more so than English, geometry, and science combined, yet we give them almost no attention. No wonder our world is in turmoil. If you don't have these skills yourself, go get them. Seek professional guidance. Friendship is far too important a skill to ignore. Without it, we risk a life of isolation.

Listen

Teach your children listening skills the old fashioned way. How, you ask? We teach listening skills by listening *to them*. There may be nothing more healing to the human spirit than to be deeply listened to by someone who cares. You don't need to jump in with a solution to every problem your child presents. You don't need to tell her that what she is doing is right or wrong. She has all she needs internally to figure stuff out. All she needs from you is a sounding board. *Listen* and *silent* have the same letters in them for a reason. Be quiet. Your children need you to look them in the eye while they talk, and they need you to listen deeply to them. The key is to manage your own anxiety when you feel like you want to jump in. You can't listen if you're thinking about your response, or worse, talking. If you can show them the art of compassionate listening, they will be healed. The experience is so powerful that they will want to pass it on. And that is how we will heal ourselves, our families, and the planet.

Follow Through

Teach your child the art and important skill of follow-through. This may sound simple, but most people do not seem to have this basic life skill. We are not running short on good intentions. We have plenty of those! But if we had a dime for every time some-one said, "I'll get back to you" and then didn't, we'd all be rich.

Some of my clients routinely come in twenty minutes late to a session only to complain about how irresponsible their children are. Focus on *your behavior* and pay attention to what you are teaching your children by your actions rather than what you say. Your children are watching you.

Homework

Is homework getting you down? Stop the power struggle. It's his life and his homework. If he doesn't want to do it, "That's okay." He just can't do anything else until he does. No TV, com-puter, play dates, dinner, soccer practice, dance class, video games, etc. Take a peaceful "it's your choice" attitude and be willing to follow through. This means that if homework isn't done, your child made the choice not to go to soccer that night. Have him call the coach personally. Let him explain why he can't make it to the game (or the party, or the practice, or wherever). Let him take personal responsibility for his choices and the con-sequences of those choices. Step aside and observe. Often, our anxiety trumps our willingness to let it all play out. Our kids are counting on that. Prove them wrong.

Waking Up

Are you having trouble getting your kid to wake up in the morning and get to breakfast on time? No worries. First, stop fighting with her. Fighting inflames the situation and gets you *both* off to a miserable start on an otherwise glorious day. Next, decide what you want from her. What time is reasonable for her to be ready to go? After you get clear, explain the new rule.

Also, let her know what the consequence will be if she breaks it. "Samantha, starting tomorrow, you will be responsible for getting yourself up and downstairs in the morning. If you aren't downstairs by 8:00 a.m., 'that's okay,' but you won't be able to go out after school. And if you miss the bus, 'that's okay,' but you won't be able to watch TV or play on the computer either. You will, however, get another chance tomorrow." If *you* can get comfortable with this approach and simply follow through without lecturing or yelling or carrying on in some way, this behavior will stop within three to five days. Typically it resolves even sooner. If you can't manage your anxiety enough to simply state the rule and consequence and follow through with no drama (yelling, lecturing, etc.), you're doomed.

Counting

Slowly counting to three when you have given a young child (two to twelve) a choice is a great tool—IF when you get to three, nothing violent occurs such as yelling, hitting, overreaction, etc. When you have arrived at three, the pre-discussed consequence must occur swiftly, with little or no comment. "I need you to stop throwing your food on the floor or dinner is over." If the child continues to throw the food, you begin counting without yelling and without a tone of frustration. In fact, the softer and more neutral the tone you can manage, the better. One (long pause), two (long pause), three. Dinner is over. Don't discuss it, just act. It's best to let her know the consequence before you start to count. Communicate the consequence in as non-threatening a tone as possible. Simply let her know what she is choosing to do—time-out, no dinner, in room, etc.—by not cooperating. If she has a fit, go take a bath.

For more on this technique, I recommend a wonderful book called *1,2,3 Magic* by Thomas Phelen.

Allowance

Allowance is a wonderful thing. But giving your children money without them having earned it teaches them nothing about how the real world works. Decide what your child needs to do to earn her allowance each day/week, and then give her the money only if she's earned it. This method teaches her that money isn't handed to you for free, which, last I checked, it isn't. Don't be angry with her because she asked for free money. I'd ask for free money too if I thought I had any chance of getting it. You can't fault her for trying. It's okay for your child to ask for whatever she wants, and it's also okay for you to say no anytime you want.

Remember that it's your job to hold the line and your child's job to push against it. If she wants to buy something, suggest she start saving her allowance. If she spends it on something you think is nonsense, "that's okay," but don't give her any more money until she has earned it. If she's out of money when her friends are going to the movies, that's what I call a bummer. Sympathize with the fact that unfortunately she can't afford to join her friends this time because she's spent all of her money. Skip the lecture. Get out of the way. This is one of those great circumstances in which your intervention is not required. All you need to do is manage your anxiety. Simply state that if she chooses to save her money, she can go next time. Communicate in a neutral tone that you hope she makes a choice to save so she has money when something comes up that's important to her. She will learn the value of money no better way.

Fair ≠ Equal

Children have different needs, personalities, and tempera-ments. That means that parents of more than one child may have to parent each child differently. Your discipline styles for each may not look the same. If that's the case, don't over-explain. Do provide a basic one-sentence explanation. It may look some-thing like this: "You and your brother are very different, so we need to respond to each of you differently." That doesn't mean general house rules will vary. Most will remain constant, such as no hitting, name-calling, wrestling, excessive treats, etc. But Johnny may need to do homework right after school, and Sally may do better after dinner. That's your call. And since you are a member of the executive parental sub-system in the family, you get to determine those choices. The kids don't get voting privi-leges this time.

It Takes a Village

Lately it seems that we have become so afraid to overstep a boundary that we have stopped helping to raise the village. It appears that the days are gone when parents looked out for chil-dren other than their own. When I was growing up, if neighbors saw me involved in something I shouldn't have been, not only did they call my parents, but they also spoke to me directly.

The other day I was walking in my neighborhood when I saw two children roughhousing in a way that was beginning to get out of hand. I stopped and said, "Hey! Knock it off!" and they did. But I have noticed that many of us don't want to get involved for fear of hurting others' feelings or butting in where we think we don't belong. GET OVER IT! These kids need us. We must be willing to step up and speak out. I am amazed when I see blatant abuse in public and people standing around doing nothing, just staring. Please, I beg of you, step out of your comfort zone and intervene in a child's life. Do it in big and small ways, but don't sit quietly when you see or hear something that feels wrong. I am not suggesting you put yourself in harm's way; I am suggesting you go find help.

Chapter Nine Take-away

If your strategies aren't working, try something new. The definition of insanity is doing the same thing over and over again and expecting different results. Don't hang onto "solutions" just because they're familiar.

ten

Commonly Asked Questions

In this chapter, I offer answers to some of the most frequently asked questions I have received from clients and Parent Power presentation participants over the years.

What if I want to jump on board with these concepts but my spouse/partner isn't interested? Won't that just confuse my child?

No. Of course, it is ideal if both parents are on board, but that doesn't always happen. I encourage you to move forward and use these strategies on your own. It is likely that your spouse will see the amazing results you're getting and want to join in. What is important is that you focus on yourself and your relationship with your child. You are fifty percent responsible for parenting your child. If *your* parenting improves, even if the other parent does nothing, your child will benefit tremendously!

Isn't this self-care approach to parenting selfish?

Actually, I believe taking a child-centered approach is selfish, not the other way around. Using your child to feel fulfilled and happy is an incredibly unfair thing to do. In my experience, this happens when parents are not willing to take responsibility and do what is necessary to find peace and happiness on their own. That is incredibly selfish. There is nothing selfish about taking responsibility for your own life and expecting your children to do the same. I call that responsible parenting.

How long do I need to follow this approach before I see changes in my child?

My answer depends on a couple of factors: 1) How long has the old pattern of parenting and resulting behaviors been in place? 2) How committed are you to change? I have seen incredible improvements occur in less than two weeks. These parents made a 180-degree turn and became very clear that the family system needed to change. They placed themselves back at the top of the hierarchy. They stopped the screaming and power struggles. They decided on the house rules, and they followed through with pre-discussed consequences without pomp or circumstance. The kids quickly got the message and thus, things turned around rapidly. These are typically younger families with kids under twelve who are still very impressionable and easy to influence. Teens can turn around quickly too, but getting through to them can involve some twists and turns along the way, which some parents can't tolerate, so they give up too soon. If parents of teens stick with it, changes can occur in as quickly as one month.

How can I "go take a bath" if my children are too young to be left alone without my constant supervision?

With all due respect, I don't accept that excuse. An infant can be put in a crib, a toddler can be put in a restricted, safe area for a fifteen-minute bath, a young child can be in his room, etc. Whatever damage you are afraid might occur if you leave your child unsupervised for a few minutes will be far worse if you stay engaged with him when he's out of control, or worse yet, *you* are out of control. Our kids will trigger our hot buttons. We need to "go take a bath" or something similar when that occurs. We can't stay and reason when we are in no state of mind to have a reasonable discussion. Figure it out. Problem-solve this one as if your relationship with your child depends on it. Because it does.

You talk a lot about the need to go to psychotherapy to work on healing myself. I can't afford therapy. Any other options?

This is tough for me to accept too, for many reasons. Over the years, many people have told me that they can't "afford" therapy, when what they really mean is that therapy is not a priority for them. I see these same people going out to dinner, driving expensive cars, going on vacations, buying their kids designer clothes, wearing expensive jewelry, etc. You get the picture. So first, I would ask you to dig deep. Are you using money as an excuse not to do this important work? Is the real reason you are avoiding therapy because you expect it to be too scary and too hard? I would say that ninety percent of the time, money is used as an excuse not to do this work. If you fall into this category, reprioritize. Go out to dinner fewer times per month, skip the vacation this year, etc. Do whatever it takes to get there. You may have to conduct a wider search than expected for a therapist who matches your needs and personality. Don't just go through your insurance company and assume that the first therapist you meet is the right one. Get referrals from friends, or if you don't want to share that you are going to therapy, get referrals from your insurance company and interview at least five therapists before you choose one.

Another less expensive option that people often don't think about is group therapy. Group therapy can be extremely effective and costs far less than individual counseling. There are also parenting classes available that can cost even less. You won't get the same individual attention in a parenting class, but attending one can go a long way in switching the focus from your child back to you, which can make a significant and beneficial shift in your family.

If you are truly in the ten percent who can't afford individual therapy, group therapy, or parenting classes, get a recommendation from a therapist for a great self-help book, and get a group of really honest people together who are also interested in doing this emotional work. Agree to hold each other accountable. Give each other homework assignments to work on each week. Follow up. Being in a group of like-minded people who are committed to their own and your emotional and spiritual growth can be enormously helpful.

Is it *always* the parents? Isn't it sometimes just the child, and the child's behavior has nothing to do with parenting? What about medicating the child? Is that ever appropriate?

Yes and no. Yes, some kids, for reasons that have nothing to do with parenting, really struggle. I truly believe that children are born with certain temperaments and personalities, and the best parenting in the world won't change that. That said, it is our responsibility to be a part of the solution for the child with challenges, not a part of the problem. So, even in circumstances that appear to have nothing to do with us or our parenting, I still believe that it is our responsibility to discover how we can help that child thrive, or how we are holding her back from reaching her full potential. We have great influence as parents, so learning to manage a challenging child benefits all. I do believe that in rare circumstances, medicating a child is appropriate and necessary for everyone's sanity. However, it should be the last resort after all other avenues have been explored and exhausted. I believe we are way over-medicating children AND parents. Again, I believe this is because our society is always looking for the quickest, cheapest solution to complicated issues.

How do I explain to my child why his friends have more toys and gadgets than he does? My kid is a straight A student and a great kid. Doesn't he deserve all those things too?

Your child deserves to feel good about his accomplishments but not be defined by them. His straight A achievement is a reflection of his hard work and dedication. Good for him! But in no way do good grades mean that your child deserves all the extra goodies that will only teach him that "stuff" is the reward for hard work. Remember, we want our kids to be intrinsically motivated, not motivated by an outside reward. Intrinsic motivation leads to lasting behavior. In addition, we need to remember that he's a great kid even if he gets a B. Even an F. He is loved even if he fails the ninth grade. Rewarding him with goodies and gadgets teaches him that your love is conditional.

I have tried all of these strategies already, and they haven't worked. Now what?

In my experience, these strategies work most of the time. If you have tried versions of them in the past, try again. The skills and approaches presented here require consistent follow-through and absolutely NO emotion. If they haven't worked in the past, I would bet that either you gave up too soon or you expressed emotion when giving out a consequence. That will blow it every time. Kids can sense if they are getting to you. If they are, the payoff of aggravating you is far more powerful than the consequence. Work on self-management. Work on getting to the root of those triggers so that a consequence is simply a consequence and isn't riddled with your emotional baggage, which only distracts the child from learning a better way.

This sounds like a great approach, but I fear a lot of judgment from family and friends. How do I deal with that?

Let me tell you something I know FOR SURE! You will be judged, and people will be crawling out of the woodwork to put you down and criticize your parenting choices. I know this from first-hand experience. They do this for one or more of the following reasons: 1) Envy (they can't manage their anxiety like you can), 2) Fear (I want to do what you are doing, but I am too afraid to do the work, or 3) Confusion (what the heck are you doing? e.g., why are you letting your child have that tantrum in public?) Ignore them. They're not ready. Resist the urge to explain or defend yourself. In my experience, that just encourages more unsolicited feedback. I find the most rewarding payoff is knowing that your child is thriving from this approach and that you are doing an excellent job preparing him to launch.

I wish I'd read a book like yours fifteen years ago. I am afraid it's too late for me. Can this strategy work for my teen? For my adult child?

It is NEVER too late. I have had many clients come to see me who have adult children (ages 21-50), and when the parent got clear about the changes that needed to happen in the relationship, so did the adult child.

What if I begin to implement these strategies and my kids get worse? Is that possible? What should I do?

It is possible that your children's behavior may intensify before calming. That is pretty normal. Remember, your children are counting on your inability to stick it out over the long haul. They are expecting you to cave. They don't trust your ability to hold the line when the going gets tough. Prove them wrong. Hang in there. Know that this burst of defiance is part of the change process, and if you can manage your anxiety long enough that your kids get the message that there's a new sheriff in town, you're golden. Take a lot of baths until this short period of intensity passes. You can do it!

Your strategies are terrific, and I wish my son would read this book. I cringe when I see how he and his spouse parent. How can I tactfully get him to read it without insulting him?

Books are great gifts. I would include the book as a gift along with other self-care items (a bath pillow and some bath salts would be great!). I would include a note stating that you've read this book and how great it was, and since they are so committed to great parenting, you just KNEW they would love it too. Remember, the only people who will read this book are those already committed to wanting to be the best parents they can be. Thus, you aren't manipulating them into learning these strategies. You are simply pointing out their strength as parents by assuming their willingness to read about it.

My teen is out of control, on drugs, and violent. I think these strategies could have worked when he was younger, but there is no way they can help now. Any advice?

Yes. Seek professional help immediately. The skills and strategies in this book will not make the kind of dent needed to get your child's attention if things have gone this far. A family intervention is needed. I would let him know that you believe something in the family has gone terribly wrong and that you all need help. A big mistake parents make is labeling the child as the identified patient in the family, which often exacerbates an already out-of-control attitude on the part of the child. Own your piece. Focus on what you may have contributed to the current state and share that with your child. Of course, he is one hundred percent responsible for his choices and consequences, but as a family, you are all in this together. Your child may not look like it, but he is scared and needs you to manage your anxiety enough to take charge, and that may include making some very difficult decisions, such as sending him to an inpatient facility while you get help for yourself.

I am successful at home implementing these strategies, but how should I handle the situation when my child has a tantrum in public?

Ignore the onlookers. Your only focus at this moment needs to be your own anxiety management and the well-being of your child. If you truly can't handle the spectators, pick up your tantruming child and move to an isolated room. My favorite places when my kids were young were a bathroom at a mall, restaurant, friend's house, etc. The other place I would often go was the car.

Whenever my kids come home from their grandparents' house, I feel like I have to start all over with them. Should I be addressing the kids or the grandparents?

Both. I have a Parent Power DVD that is a great tool to give to caretakers. It can be purchased at www.parentassist.net/dvd. It's a fun, funny presentation that explains these concepts in a way that everyone can understand and get on board with! Another option is to have a proactive, rather than a reactive, conversation with your parents or in-laws. Explain the approach you are taking with your child and how much you would appreciate their help. You will be amazed at how impactful a discussion like this can be. I would also explain to your children what the expected behavior is wherever they are, and what the consequences will be if that behavior doesn't occur. Bottom line is that I would address this issue calmly and proactively from both sides.

You're a therapist, parenting coach, AND a health and wellness coach? How is health and wellness related to therapy or parenting?

We are whole people, not just parents, and not just emotional beings. Through my own personal journey to wellness, I realized that no matter how committed I was to my own emotional and spiritual growth, if I wasn't feeling well physically, I wasn't feeling well period. As I watched my clients struggle to get themselves better emotionally and spiritually, I noticed them struggling with physical issues too, and I could see that these physical issues were interfering with their ability to implement these strategies. It's hard to follow through with the recommendations described in this book when you are feeling physically well, but it's almost impossible when you are nutritionally depleted, fatigued, or carrying excess weight. As a result, I started on a journey to find the best, clearest path to physical wellness, and that journey led me to a great company called Team Beachbody. This is the company that makes Shakeology, which I refer to in the book as my daily dose of dense nutrition. I became involved with Team Beachbody to help myself first and my clients second. As my clients started to address their physical vulnerabilities, they became far more prepared and energized to take on the challenges of parenting well. Discovering this company and the products they offer has been life-changing for me, my family, and many of my clients. If you feel that your physical state gets in the way of living your best life, check out Shakeology and the fitness programs Team Beachbody offers at www.beachbodycoach.com/kevnec, or contact me directly at robin@parentassist.net if you have questions. One thing I know for sure: a parent who feels physically well is a less cranky one. I am grateful that I am able to offer these products to my family and friends, and as a value-added service to my clients.

When I was a kid my parents "put themselves first," and I felt unloved, rejected, and abandoned. I don't want my kids to feel

that way. What's the difference between the neglect I felt as a kid and your self-care approach?

These two parenting styles are completely different. In previous generations, many parents gave very little thought to parenting. They were acting on impulse and doing whatever felt right at the moment. There was very little conscious parenting, and even less self-care-focused parenting. I want you to put your own needs first, but I am not suggesting you ignore your children. I want you to love and respect your children with every fiber of your being. Talk to them, spend time with them, laugh with them, and make memories with them. I want you to spend quality time on the patio, deck, or porch together, eat dinner as a family, take family vacations, and ask about their day, every day. But I also want you to teach them to ask you about YOUR day, because YOUR day is also important. And I want you to have a day that is filled with joy and adventure to tell them about. I don't want your answer to begin and end with "laundry" or "hanging around until you got home." Can you see the difference?

Additionally, have you thought about what things will be like when your kids have left home? If you have not focused on your own interests and created a life for yourself, what will you do then? If you haven't spent time nurturing other important relationships, with whom will you spend your time?

I was in therapy before and didn't have a positive experience. I felt so uncomfortable. I want to be a good parent, but I don't like looking at my past and remembering feelings and events I'd rather forget. Why can't I learn parenting skills without needing to dredge up the past?

This question hits the nail on the head as to why most people don't participate in the hard work of therapy—it's uncomfortable! And as a species, we try to avoid being uncomfortable at all costs. It is the same reason many don't exercise. I wish I could tell you that there is a way around it. If there were one, I would have used it myself. But the truth is that you must be willing to endure the discomfort if you want to change. It may not be necessary to explore every aspect of a less-than-ideal childhood, but it is necessary to look at the parts of your childhood that are affecting your parenting. By looking at them, processing them, and thinking about them differently, you can break the cycle of that pattern that has caused you pain. By being willing to be uncomfortable, you may be saving your children a lifetime of sorrow. It's worth it!

As I was reading your book, I was thinking about other important relationships in my life where these strategies might be helpful. Do these strategies apply to non-parenting relationships as well?

Congratulations on your discovery! YES! YES! and YES! You can use everything discussed in this book to improve all of your relationships. Think about it. What relationship wouldn't improve if you focused on managing your own anxiety instead of trying to manage the other person's behavior? How could it hurt to "go take a bath" when you are feeling at your wits' end with your husband, best friend, or sibling? This book really addresses how to master the art of self-management, and once you have done that, you have mastered the art of being in relationships. Good for you!

eleven

Managing Parental Anxiety: The Good, the Bad, and the Ugly

Love yourself first, and everything else falls in line.
~ Lucille Ball

I have talked extensively about anxiety management in this book. However, you may still be wondering how your parental anxiety and unaddressed personal issues directly affect the parenting choices you make that interfere with your child's development. I hope that the following stories will help you understand why effective parenting is intricately linked to your ability to manage anxiety. These examples demonstrate the differences between conscious, deliberate, thoughtful parenting (the good), knee-jerk, thoughtless, unconscious parenting (the bad), and show how unresolved personal issues negatively impact your parenting choices in profound ways (the ugly). *Names and details have been changed to protect identities.*

The Good

Many years ago, I was working with an eighteen-year-old young man named George, who was addicted to cocaine. After working with me for some time, George became sober and his life began to improve greatly. He and his family were thrilled. He deepened his relationship with a long-time girlfriend, his family relationships improved significantly as trust was restored, and his professional life skyrocketed. Life was going very well for this family until Christmas Day, 2007.

I was at home that day when I received an emergency call from George's mother. She told me that George had relapsed and showed up to Christmas dinner high on cocaine. Their first call was to a cousin who was in Narcotics Anonymous. The cousin told Mom not to let George in the house for Christmas dinner, and not to allow him back in the house at all until he received treatment. This was especially difficult because George lived at home and had nowhere else to go. It didn't help anyone's anxiety level that it was cold and it was Christmas. Mom was understandably shaken and confused, so she called me for a second opinion. I knew not letting George back home was the right choice, but even my anxiety increased at the thought of George alone on the streets in the cold on Christmas with nowhere to go. Still, here his mother was on the phone asking me as the professional how to proceed.

I took a deep breath and told her the truth. I said, "Mrs. Smith, the greatest chance your son has at recovery is for you to allow natural and logical consequences to affect him. I suggest you let him feel the consequence of the choice he just made to relapse. I agree with your cousin not to allow him back home until he receives treatment." I could hear her start to sob. She simply said "Okay," and we hung up.

Mom did exactly what she was advised to do. As a result of George's mom putting her own anxiety and sadness aside and doing what her son most needed, I am happy to report that George went directly to treatment that evening. And I am even happier to report that he is still sober today—married with kids!

I know managing anxiety is super hard, and I know very few of us could do what George's mom did. In fact, most parents "in the name of love" would allow him back in the house. It was Christmas, after all! I also know that the large majority of those children "let back in" will remain addicted. Sadly, untreated addiction ends in only three ways: jail, institutions, or death. This is why if we can allow our children to feel the consequences as often and as early as possible, we help them achieve the greatest quality of life possible. It is LOVING to make these tough calls. It is the most loving, courageous, helpful thing to do to allow your kids to suffer the consequences of bad choices—even if those consequences are as intense as jail, inpatient treatment, or losing their driver's license for unpaid speeding tickets or DUI charges. Putting our children on the right path starts small by allowing them to accept a detention or deal with a loss of phone privileges or decline an invitation to a party because of their disrespectful tone. Good parenting requires enormous anxiety management, and anxiety management is only possible with self-discipline and a lot of personal work. It also helps if we take a lot of baths, soaking ourselves in a pool of self-care. It also takes courage, and I know you have the courage because you are still reading this book!

The Bad

One day when my older daughter, Arli, was five and my younger daughter, Zoe, was two, I suggested to my husband that

I go out to get us some ice cream for dessert (long before my vegan days). I said that I would take Arli with me and would leave Zoe home with him. Zoe and my husband were happily playing in the basement, and it felt unnecessary to schlep Zoe with us, car seat and all, just to pick up ice cream that I was bringing home anyway.

When I was ready to leave, I asked Arli if she wanted to come with me. She screamed "YES!" As we were putting our coats on, I told her that we were going by ourselves, and that Zoe was playing downstairs with Daddy and did not need to know we were leaving because she would want to come. "Okay!" she said as she walked over to the basement door, opened it, and screamed, "Zoe!!! Me and Mommy are going out to get some ice cream now and we will be back soon with it. Don't cry, okay?" As you can predict, Zoe immediately started to cry and insist that she wanted to come too, creating a lot of unnecessary drama for all.

I was stunned! I could not believe the defiance. It wasn't like Arli could have forgotten what I'd said. I had just said it, and within seconds she'd gone over to the basement door and done the exact opposite of what I had asked her to do. I was *really* angry. So what did I do? I did what any reasonable parenting coach would do (insert sarcastic tone here): I said "Let's go!" and I lectured her in the car all the way to Baskin Robbins *where she was going to get ice cream.* Just ridiculous.

As we were driving and I was lecturing, I was aware of the dead silence coming from the backseat. It was at that moment that I realized it must really be upsetting to hear me speak to her this way. "Let me see what's going on," I thought. So I moved the rearview mirror to see her. I was sure that I had humiliated her and that she felt ashamed by her behavior so I was actually starting to feel quite awful. However, much to my surprise, she was not looking sad or ashamed or sorry at all. She looked bored!

She wasn't even listening to me. She was playing with her fingernails, and if I could have captioned her thoughts, they would have been, "When is this bitch gonna shut up and give me my ice cream?!!" She didn't care that I was lecturing her; she cared only about getting her ice cream. My "punishment" of lecturing was teaching her NOTHING except to get really good at tuning me out. Sound familiar?

It wasn't until days later that I realized where I'd gone wrong. Imagine the same scenario except without the lecture. Instead, what if I had simply said, "Oh, I see by your choice to tell Zoe we were going for ice cream after I told you not to that you have decided not to have ice cream tonight"? Then, off I would have gone to get ice cream for three (me, hubby, Zoe) instead of four. Wouldn't that have been a better lesson in listening? Then she would have learned that when you don't listen, you don't get what you want. No yelling, anger, or lecturing necessary—just no ice cream. I guarantee that behavior would have never occurred again if I had been conscious enough to think it through and follow through with that logical consequence rather than carrying on with a lecture about not listening to Mommy.

When I tell this story in my parenting presentations, the audience GASPS! "You would have withheld the ice cream? You would have eaten it IN FRONT OF HER? That's sooooooo cruel!" participants say. Seriously, that's the response I routinely get. But if we can't manage our anxiety about a one-time ice cream withdrawal, how will we ever be able to do it when more serious issues arise, as in George's case? We need to get a grip. Parents react to my ice cream story as if I'd just beaten my daughter with a sledgehammer. It's a crazy, over-the-top reaction, and I get it consistently.

We must learn to manage our anxiety if we want our kids to have a fighting chance at learning self-discipline and lead a successful life. There will be more opportunities for ice cream. But I want my child to learn that I say what I mean and I mean what I say. My wish is that I had thought of it at the time instead of reacting in an unconscious, knee-jerk fashion. You see, I'm a work in progress too! But you can bet that the next time a similar situation occurred (and it did), I was ready! ☺

The Ugly

The situation I am about to describe was the only time in my career I was rendered speechless. Prepare yourself.

Jordan was addicted to heroin, and by the age of sixteen, he had been in and out of an astonishing twelve rehabilitation facilities. At sixteen! I could not imagine what was happening with this child or within the family that was causing Jordan to chronically relapse. I soon found out.

I started working with Jordan in the spring of 2004, and together we developed a plan to achieve and maintain sobriety. I worked with the family to see if I could assess whether there was something within the family system that was causing him to relapse time and again. However, I found nothing. The family showed genuine concern for Jordan, and I could see no overt enabling behaviors or red flags that could have triggered his many relapses.

Jordan followed our mutually developed plan and achieved sobriety quickly. This wasn't unusual for him, as he had achieved sobriety many times before through various treatment programs, but rarely maintained his sobriety for more than three months post-treatment. I was thrilled when we got to the one-year sobriety mark. He was thrilled too, and his family was overjoyed. As a result, I asked Jordan's parents to join us for a session to devise a sobriety maintenance plan. They agreed.

When Jordan and his family arrived at my office for that post one-year-sobriety session, I could feel tension in the air emanating from the waiting room. When they walked into my office, I immediately asked what was going on. The family and Jordan reported that he had relapsed just a few days after his one-year sobriety anniversary. I was shocked and dumbfounded (but not yet speechless).

As I inquired further about what had led to the relapse, I was informed that Jordan's parents had thrown him a one-year sobriety party, *complete with alcohol!!* This was when I became speechless, and suddenly it was clear why Jordan was unable to maintain sobriety after his numerous bouts in rehab. Suddenly the clouds had parted and I could see clearly. I could see, but I could not speak. It felt like hours before I could say anything, but I imagine it was only a few minutes. When I uttered a sound, it was simply to ask "Why?" Jordan's parents explained that it was far too upsetting to imagine their son as a recovering addict. They wanted desperately to have a "normal" son, and since he had stayed sober for an entire year, it seemed like the right time to see if he could use alcohol socially. *This made perfect sense to them.* Dad justified their actions by reminding me that alcohol was not Jordan's drug of choice; heroin was. They wanted him off heroin, not alcohol. They desperately wanted a son who was "normal," not a "recovering addict." Their need to have a "normal" son mattered far more to them than what their son actually needed, which was to live a sober life. (I'm sure they weren't conscious of that, though.) Despite the clear messages they had received from countless rehabilitation centers, and me—that their son must abstain from all types of drugs, including alcohol, in order to remain sober—they sabotaged his efforts. In spite of the devastating consequences, they defended their position throughout the session, and once again, Jordan was back to square one.

I don't remember anything after that session. I'm not sure if they left treatment or if I have blocked the aftermath out of my mind as a form of self-protection. I do know that unless Jordan's parents get their OWN help, Jordan will have little chance of life-long sobriety. He will likely remain addicted, and as I mentioned earlier, that will end in jail, institutions, or death. Jordan (and his family) had already felt devastating consequences from his addiction—including being ostracized by peers and extended family, thrown out of school, and arrested multiple times. He was scheduled to be released from juvenile probation at the time of the relapse, but of course, he stayed on probation.

This story is heartbreaking. Jordan had his whole life ahead of him. Unless he matures super-quick and gets a clue fast that his family is creating roadblocks to his success, he has little to no hope of sobriety. Ultimately, Jordan alone is responsible for his choice to relapse. But do you think his family was part of the problem or part of the solution? Don't we as parents want to be part of the solution when our kids are struggling? Jordan's family clearly had an unconscious investment in keeping him sick and dependent on them. Their unresolved issues were wreaking havoc with his life.

While this may seem like an extreme example, and it is in many ways, this type of behavior happens all the time in families. Parents who claim to live for their children—putting children at the top of the hierarchy—are the biggest offenders. These parents, who are overly focused on their children and concerned about how they look to the community, set their children up for a lifetime of pain. People claim that a self-care parenting style is selfish? Quite the opposite. An overly child-focused parenting style is as selfish as it gets—and destructive. In this case, Jordan's parents could not see how their issues and anxiety were preventing Jordan from getting sober. In many other less intense cases, parents can't see how their anxiety blocks a child's growth and development. I see it clearly, every day.

You have an opportunity to stop this cycle by getting out of the way of your children's development. Let them feel the consequences of their actions. Support them if they try to improve their lives, even if you perceive that this makes you look "bad" to others. Get the alcohol out of the house if your child has a drinking problem. Let your son or daughter go to the college of their choosing, or no college at all if that is their choice. Let your child experience life and the consequences that follow if he makes a poor choice. Don't get him an attorney to soften the consequences—let him feel them! Support his desire for independence when opportunities arise. This will help launch him into adulthood. Being an adult isn't easy. Don't pretend that it is. Get whatever help and support you need to allow this to happen. There is no greater investment you can make.

twelve
Conclusion

I have worked as a licensed psychotherapist and parenting coach for nearly twenty-five years. One thing I know for sure, after meeting with hundreds of families, is that you get the exact child you most need in your life—not necessarily the one you expected. In my opinion, children are perfectly matched to parents in order for the parents to work on the very issues with which they most struggle. Our kids have an inherent ability to find the issue we are most sensitive to and lay on it for as long as it is necessary for us to see that this is OUR issue, not theirs. Once we recognize that we own the issue, it is our responsibility to work to resolve it. When we get clear that we are the ones who need to change and grow, our children are released from the burden we have placed on them. As we work on our issues, their behavior usually shifts or stops. This is why I work only with parents, not children: *we* pass on *our* unhealed emotional wounds to our kids to resolve. Their behavior doesn't come from nowhere; it comes from us. I encourage you to shift the focus and work with a professional to heal yourself. If you change your approach and stop looking at your child as the one with the issue, you will be amazed at the results.

Although peer pressure can be tough and has a huge influence on our children, it is not nearly as powerful as the influence that we have as parents. Even when you are utterly convinced (as

I have been) that your kids couldn't care less what you think, you're wrong. They care a great deal. And while they may not always act in a way that appears to validate this fact, it's true. So make your family values known. Send clear, consistent messages and take deep breaths and a lot of baths! Step back and trust the process.

I know that the concepts, strategies, and tips I have suggested throughout this book can be very hard to implement. Conscious parenting with a self-care focus is not for the faint of heart. It's much easier to blame your child and send her to therapy than to take a deeper look at yourself. It's easier to yell and get angry with her than it is to manage your own anxiety. Sometimes it's easier to say no than to work out the details that come along with a yes. I totally get it. I struggle with the same things—every day—and on some days, hourly. I promise you this: if you can adopt this approach, you will feel a sense of satisfaction, joy, and accomplishment that is like nothing else. The bliss you will get from raising independent, self-sufficient, healthy kids will be better than any high out there. Take the plunge. Take the leap of faith. Breathe. Dive into this important work. I can't guarantee that it will always be easy, but I can assure you that it will be worth it.

Still unsure? I encourage you to take a moment and remember yourself at your child's age. Think about how you experienced your own parents. Did you experience them as loving, warm, fun, and joyous? Or did you experience them as short-tempered, angry, demanding, frustrated, or ambivalent? Did they LOVE their life? Did you experience them as happy, balanced people? After you have the answer to these questions in your mind, imagine how your life might have been different if your parents had picked up this book when you were your child's age. Imagine if they had taken the suggestions seriously and immersed themselves in a pool of self-care. Would your childhood experience have been any different? More peaceful? Easier? More relaxed? Would your life look different today? Would you have made different choices? Once you have the answers to these questions, you will know that this journey of self-care and self-discovery is worth it. For me and all the brave parents who have chosen to take this courageous journey, I know it is. Children who are raised with this style of parenting typically blossom into confident, self-reliant, joyous, independent, loving adults. I don't know about you, but that's my greatest wish for my children. I feel confident that when I am in my final years of this life, I will look back and care about little else besides the legacy of love I have left behind. For that, and for so many other reasons, I'm taking the road less travelled. I hope you'll join me.

Remember: world peace is achieved one healed parent at a time.

Our deepest fear is not that we are inadequate. Our deepest fear is that we are powerful beyond measure. It is our light, not our darkness, that most frightens us. We ask ourselves, "Who am I to be brilliant, gorgeous, talented, fabulous?" Actually, who are you not to be? You are a child of God. Your playing small does not serve the world. There is nothing enlightened about shrinking so that other people won't feel insecure around you. We are all meant to shine, as children do. We were born to make manifest the glory of God that is within us. It's not just in some of us; it's in everyone. And as we let our own light shine, we unconsciously give other people permission to do the same. As we are liberated from our own fear, our presence automatically liberates others.

~Marianne Williamson, *A Return to Love: Reflections on the Principles of "A Course in Miracles"*

About the Author

Robin M. Kevles-Necowitz, M.Ed., LPC, is a licensed professional counselor and parenting coach in Fairless Hills, Pennsylvania. She has been in private practice working with adults, couples, and families for nearly twenty-five years. She also works as an Independent Team Beachbody Coach (www.beachbodycoach.com/kevnec). As a wellness coach, she supports others in achieving greater health through fitness and nutrition. She lives in Yardley, Pennsylvania with her husband, two daughters, and dog, "Nugget Necowitz." Her parenting coaching website is www.ParentAssist.net, and she can also be found on Facebook by searching for Parent Assist.

23977404R10098

Made in the USA
Charleston, SC
08 November 2013